# *San Pedro River Review*

Vol. 9 No. 1          Spring 2017

# San Pedro River Review
## Vol. 9 No. 1          Spring 2017

San Pedro River Review (SPRR) Vol. 9 No. 1, Spring 2017
Blue Horse Press, Redondo Beach, California, United States.

Front cover: *Between Black Butte and Kane Wash, Mojave Desert*. Back cover: *Approaching China Lake*. Photos courtesy of Blue Horse Press Archives (2015, 2016).

EDITORS & PUBLISHERS: Jeffrey and Tobi Alfier

SPRR (ISSN 1944-5954) is a semiannual publication of poetry and art, published by Blue Horse Press. The website associated with SPRR is www.bluehorsepress.com.  All rights reserved ©

SPRR is indexed in the University of Wisconsin-Madison Special Collections Little Magazines unit and the International Directory of Little Magazines & Small Presses. It appears in the holdings of the University of Arizona Poetry Center, Texas State University and Baylor University. SPRR also appears in the EBSCO research database.

[clmp]

Community of Literary Magazines & Presses

# TABLE OF CONTENTS

**Feature Interview:**

SPRR with Anders Carlson-Wee and Kai Carlson-Wee

**Poetry:**

**Art:**

One should always go toward the place for which there is no sign.

Henry Miller, *Black Spring*

# INTERVIEW with Anders Carlson-Wee
# and Kai Carlson-Wee

**Anders Carlson-Wee** is a 2015 NEA Fellow and author of *Dynamite* (2015), and co-author, with his brother Kai, of *Two-Headed Boy*, which won the David Blair Memorial Chapbook Prize (2016), as well as *mercy songs* (2016). Publication credits include *Ploughshares*, *New England Review*, *AGNI*, *Poetry Daily*, *The Missouri Review*, *Best New Poets*, *Best American Nonrequired Reading*, and *Narrative*. He is winner of the Frost Place Chapbook Prize, the *Ninth Letter*'s Poetry Award, *New Delta Review*'s Editors' Prize, and was runner-up for the 2016 Discovery/*Boston Review* Poetry Prize. At present, he is a 2016 McKnight Fellow.

**Kai Carlson-Wee** received a BA in English from the University of Minnesota and an MFA in Creative Writing from the University of Wisconsin-Madison. He has received fellowships and awards from the MacDowell Colony, the Breadloaf Writer's Conference, the Sewanee Writer's Conference, the Dorothy Sargent Rosenberg Fund, and his work has appeared in journals such as *Narrative Magazine*, *Best New Poets*, *Poetry Northwest*, *TriQuarterly*, *Gulf Coast*, and *The Missouri Review*, which selected a group of his poems for their 2013 Editor's Prize. A former Wallace Stegner Fellow, he lives in San Francisco, and is a Jones Lecturer in poetry at Stanford University. He is co-author, with his brother Anders, of *Two-Headed Boy*, which won the David Blair Memorial Chapbook Prize (2016), as well as *mercy songs* (2016). Most recently, his poem "Crystal Meth" was chosen by Nick Flynn as runner-up for the *Third Coast Literary Magazine* Poetry Prize.

~

SPRR: To you both, we appreciate very much your acceptance of our interview offer, especially for our Back Roads & Byways-themed issue. For us, our theme resonates quite well with what we find in your poetry. I first came across your work in *Narrative*. When I read those poems for the first time, I told Tobi, my co-editor, "You gotta read these guys. And they hang around trains, as well!" From there it was a matter of seeking more of your poetry to read, as well as reading interviews with you.

SPRR: First off, congratulations on your recent publications, *mercy songs* and *Dynamite*. How are the sales going?

Kai: Thanks, Jeff! We've been on a lucky streak with chapbooks this year. I don't how this happened but Anders and I published three collaborative projects since April: *mercy songs* (Diode Editions), *Northern Corn* (Upper Rubber Boot), and *Two-Headed Boy* (Organic Weapon Arts), which we sent around for a year-and-a-half before anyone batted an eye. Crazy it all seemed to happen at once, but sales have been good!

SPRR: *Riding the Highline* is another project I'm quite excited about. I've seen your Facebook notices about the festivals and awards the film's earned. Is there a release date for the public at large to see it?

Anders: It's live! You can watch it online here: www.ridingthehighline.com

Kai: When we made *Riding the Highline* we never thought it would get into film festivals. We figured maybe a few poets would watch it and get excited about taking a road trip. We never thought it would snowball the way it did. I guess we kind of got lucky with AWP allowing us to premiere the film in Minneapolis, and then the reception it had at the Napa Valley Film Festival, which was so unexpected. One night we were hanging with John Travolta, drinking bottomless glasses of wine, walking through rooms made of roses, and the next night we were going on stage to receive an award and give an acceptance speech. It felt very Hollywood and over-the-top, but there was energy there, there was real enthusiasm. The crowds were ignited by something beyond the circumstance and celebrity. Writing poetry can be so boring sometimes: judgment flying everywhere, people trying to cling to some prize, some minor reputation. It gets tiring. I'm not saying I wish the poetry world were more like Hollywood, I'm saying the tone could be more supportive and celebratory. Less cagy and hierarchical. I know some of this is related to money and general public interest, but I think if younger poets were given more opportunities to publish books, the interest would grow and the money would start to show up.

Since Napa we've screened at a number of big festivals across the country—Arizona International, Minneapolis International, San Francisco Doc Fest—and each has been a serious honor. I think the coolest part has been the audience's reaction to seeing poetry on the big screen. There are a number of documentary films about older poets or dead poets, but there aren't so many about young poets living their lives, making contemporary work, doing cool things. In 1959 there was a film made by Robert Frank, Allen Ginsberg, and Jack Kerouac called "Pull My Daisy," which is a pretty good film and shows them as they lived. You see their apartments, their mannerisms. Frank Stanford made a film called "It Wasn't a Dream, It Was a Flood," but I've never seen it cause there are only a few surviving copies. Matthew Dickman helped write a superbowl commercial a few years back. These projects are considered minor experiments and nobody talks about them, but they are attempts to bring poetry to a larger audience and to capture a slice of the vision these writers were after. How cool would it be if Kerouac would have brought a video camera on the road, or if Carolyn Forche would have worked with a director to bring "The Country Between Us" to life? Part of the problem a public audience has with poetry is the abstraction, its lack of narrative and character. Some writers solve this by writing prose and breaking the lines, some write hallmark cards and post them to Instagram, some writers work off their personal identities, some writers start writing songs instead of poems, ala Leonard Cohen. I think multimedia, and film in particular, has a lot to offer poetry, and I think we'll see a shift in the next fifty years. Not in the direction of Hollywood exactly, but in forms that translate well to the internet.

**SPRR: Writers are always asked about their influences. Can you trace any particular influences of your poetry?**

**Kai:** When I think of influences I go back to music. I wrote poems growing up, but I wasn't entirely sold on poetry. I was more drawn to lyrics by songwriters like Bob Dylan, Kurt Cobain, Joni Mitchell, Neil Young. Over the years I've been influenced by musicians and artists as much as I have been by poets. If I were only drawing influence from poets, I don't think I would write the way I do. I would probably be more publishable, but I wouldn't be willing to imagine my work in a larger context. Poetry is famous for being insular, and I think that tendency is one of the big things holding it back right now. I don't want to place blame, but I think older poets have done a disservice to the younger generation by couching themselves so exclusively in the academy. They've developed as teachers and careerists instead of as artists. If you look at the structure of MFA programs and conferences, they operate on a hierarchical system that keeps older published authors at the top, and younger unpublished authors at the bottom. The problem is that this puts pressure on young poets to be hirable, to be acceptable in an MFA setting. As a result, they end up writing for an older audience. This has a tendency to make the work conservative and predictable. When I started writing poetry I felt this vibe and I wanted to develop a style that spoke to a younger audience. I wanted to write the kind of poetry I wasn't able to find when I was in my twenties, in college. I wanted to honor the impulse of poetry, rather than the security of my ego, if that makes sense. When I look at my own personal influences—Yeats, Whitman, Roethke, Plath, Bly, Levis—I see a common thread of imagery, experience, accessibility, and a willingness to be wild, to be a little unhinged. Influence is essential, but I think if poetry is going to survive and appeal to younger generations, it needs to look outside itself. It needs to exist in a broader culture and it needs to be willing to fail.

**SPRR: When did your impressions of the world first emerge through poetry? What drew you to poetry as your primary genre?**

**Kai:** My first poems were love poems. That's how it started. When I was in elementary school I wrote poems to girls I had crushes on. I would spend weeks on these short little ten-line poems and leave them anonymously in their desks. It was a very earnest thing, and the poems were terrible, but they were sincere. I don't know if I should tell this story, but there was a girl in my fourth grade class named Jill, and I wrote her a poem for the last day of school and left it in her cubbie in the hall. The poem was maybe eight lines long and I think I compared her hair to wheat fields and her eyes to summer skies. Slightly objectifying, but it was sweet. After school got out for the year I sort of forgot about the poem, thinking she didn't care or it was cheesy. I probably assumed she didn't even find it. A few years later, my family moved to Fargo, North Dakota, and during my sophomore year of high school I traveled with our church's youth group down to New Orleans. They were having an ELCA gathering of Lutheran youth groups from across the country and thousands of kids were down there, running around the Superdome, praising God. At some point I bumped into the group from my old church and they wanted to hang out. We went to their hotel room to ditch the church stuff and surprisingly, this girl Jill was there. We started reminiscing about old times as kids and she asked me to go into the bathroom to smoke a cigarette. For some reason everyone was smoking Newport Menthols at the time and she pulled out some Newports and stuffed a towel under the door so the smoke would get sucked up the fan. I was looking at her back and I saw her shoulders slump down and she started to breathe heavy. I was like, *Jill, are you okay?* and she turned around with tears in her eyes. I said, *What's going on? Are you okay?* and she said, *I have to ask you something. Did you write a poem for me in fourth grade?* I was sort of embarrassed about it and tried to deny the whole thing. But she said, *Look, I know it was you who wrote the poem.* After a minute I sheepishly admitted that it was true. She then began to recite the whole poem from memory. She knew every line, as if it were one of the prayers we'd been reciting at the gathering. I was blown away. We sat there in the hotel bathroom smoking these menthols and there was this electric connection between us. I can't remember what happened next. I think we kissed, but it almost didn't matter. I just couldn't believe that someone had carried a poem I wrote inside their mind. How real it felt between us then. It was the first time I felt how powerful a poem could be. It was wild. I'll never forget that moment.

**SPRR: I've got a notebook I carry in my back pocket, just for spontaneous thoughts that need to be written down. How do you get it on the page – notebook or computer?**

**Anders:** I hear the words in my head first, and I usually edit at that stage for voice and music before I ever write them down. So my writing is for sound first, before it ever becomes a visual. Next I handwrite in a notebook, for several reasons: 1) because it makes the writing process more physical and grounded; 2) because this way it's written in "my hand," which is sloppy and misspelled and dark from pressing hard against the paper, and is therefore mine; 3) because I like to make lines and arrows and symbols that you can't make on a computer screen; 4) because words typed and formatted on a screen in an appealing font already look finished; 5) because a computer has access to so much else, and while I'm writing a first draft I want to be completely absorbed, with no possibility for distraction; and 6) because I already spend enough time on a screen.

**Kai:** I started carrying a moleskin around with me when I was living in San Diego back in 2001. This was before I went to college and started thinking of myself as a writer. I would jot down thoughts, fragments of speech, ideas for skate tricks, logos of made-up companies I wanted to start. The moleskin became a necessary accessory, sort of like smart phones are for most people today. When I got to college I spent a year studying abroad at Oxford and was often traveling through foreign cities, wandering from station to station, lonely and feeling like a stranger. I got in the habit of using my journal as a travelogue, writing down everything I saw and felt in the moment. I was reading Wordsworth and Whitman at the time and I was interested in spontaneous emotion and all that. Inscape. Inspiration. Not exactly a 'first thought best thought' kind of thing, but a *living experience* kind of thing. I probably wrote three to four poems a day and was obsessed with developing an original style. I wanted to create a poem that was propelled by a spiritual engine, that reflected the rhythm and action of life, but was able to somehow transcend it. The journal was a huge part of this project. Now if I leave the house without something to write on I get nervous. I panic a little bit. The best poems seem to come to me when I'm on my feet, traveling from one place to the next, in a state of transition and movement. Something about spontaneous language feels more real and authentic to me than language I use for specific effects. I might only get a few lines this way, but they will usually be the skeleton of the poem I write later. Almost all my poems are written this way.

**SPRR: Some believe that one has to write every day otherwise their creative abilities atrophy. I never found this to be the case, and can't imagine myself having a designated time each day to write. It comes when it comes. How do you feel about that?**

**Anders:** I'm a worker. I don't do well with waiting for inspiration. I write almost every day, for 4-6 hours, at cafes. Most days I honestly don't get that much done. I'll try to start a new poem and it'll come out pretty bad. Then I'll edit something I already wrote and the effort will amount to revising a handful of lines. Writing is slow work. But the daily grind works for me: I keep track of all my drafts, and I can trace every one of my finished poems back to a bad draft that I wrote on a mediocre day at the cafe. Sunflowers grow tall on a diet of compost, you could say. But most of what I write never breaks through the surface, just stays in my notebook. I think of all that abandoned writing as practice, and also as a junkyard for me to pick through later for parts (mixing my metaphors, I know).

I'll also say that Kai and I grew up skating, and compared to artists, skaters have a more practical sense of inspiration and work habits. In skate culture, you just get up and go skating; you get busy, no hesitation, no questions asked. And since skating is location-specific and semi-illegal, it's more in the moment: *Do your trick now, before the cops get here, or it'll never happen. Now or never.* So there's an immediacy; time is working against you in a very real way. So, as a skater, I got used to working hard, channeling all my energy into the moment, and I've kept up that practice as a writer.

**SPRR: For us, one of the captivating features of your poetry is its strong narrative that pulls us in as readers, holding us to the page. There are no wasted words, a strength of concision that sharpens the images. This is a difficult thing to do because in our daily speech we don't police what we say as far as unnecessary articles, etc. Seems the imagination we exercise as poets must undergird image and lyric in order to sustain the momentum of the poem.**

**Anders:** A lot of my poems are action-based scenes with a survival element. This style of poem grew out of my interest in wilderness survival and train hopping, which both put you into a kind of survival mode. In survival training, the first thing you learn is that nothing can be wasted: not time, not energy, not water, not food, not warmth—nothing. And not only that, but everything must serve multiple purposes: a shirt is still a shirt, but is also raw material for shade, bandage, and water collection; a rock is also a knife; two sticks are also a splint; your voice is also a birdcall; your fire is also a signal; etc. In that mindset, there's little room for imagination that expands outwards toward what is not there; rather, the imagination turns inward, reexamining what *is* there, finding ways to make it more, make it new. In those poems, I've worked hard to strip the craft down to the bare essentials, so the form will mimic the mindset and story of the poem.

**Kai:** I have a complicated relationship with narrative. I'm not really interested in creating fictional stories in my poems, but I *am* interested in writing collections that feel like novels, that have a narrative arc in place. I tend to imagine poems the same way I imagine documentary filmmaking—allowing for accidents to happen, spontaneous moments, etc. This is more of a *reactive* way of making art, where the narrative develops as the experience unfolds, as the poem is being written, rather than the other way around. Most of the poetry I associate with 'narrative poetry' feels soft to me, and forcibly constructed. I get the feeling of a story but not of an experience, not of a *true* experience, and the poetry feels thin. Basically, I don't want to be chained to the history of my life. I'm interested in exploring my autobiography, but in a way that abandons fact and approaches myth. When you make a documentary film you are always reacting to inspiration, to something that catches your eye or ear in the moment, and the job of editing is really a matter of imagining the narrative potential of scattered spontaneous scenes. When jazz musicians work off a riff they are doing a similar thing. When C.D Wright wrote *Deepstep Come Shining*, when Lou Reed improvised lyrics, when Gary Winogrand took street photos, the idea of narrative was not the central goal, but a narrative quality still came through. I'm definitely invested in narrative work, and I'm always thinking about what the story is when I sit down to write a poem, but I want the narrative to allow for improvisation, for the muse and lightning touch. I want the scenes to build narrative strength, but to range over a whole collection, rather than a single poem.

**SPRR: Kai, would you tell us a bit about being a Jones Lecturer?**

**Kai:** Well, I did a Wallace Stegner Fellowship at Stanford a couple years ago, and the Jones Lectureship is sort of a continuation of the fellowship. I've been doing it for the last four years now. It's a very generous position, and I'm extremely grateful to the students I've taught over the years for putting up with my shenanigans and trusting me with their work. I know some writers complain about having to teach, but I really enjoy it. There's an enthusiasm for writing you don't really find outside the classroom. I still remember the first time I read Levis, the first time I read Crush by Richard Siken, or Song by Brigit Pegeen Kelly. Those moments were big openings in my poetry, my understanding of what a poem could be, and it's just super exciting to be able to share that feeling with young writers.

At Stanford I teach a few different classes, but my favorite is a class Eavan Boland encouraged me to teach called *The American Road Trip*. It's built around journeys and literature of the road. We talk about the history of 'road stories' in America and what they mean to American identity. You would love it, Jeff! We look at classics like *On the Road* and *The Cremation of Sam McGee*, but we also look at a non-traditional road narrative and compare them across mediums. We look at stories by Flannery O'Conner and compare them to films like Badlands by Terrence Malick. Photos from civil rights protests in the south and compare them to what's currently happening at Standing Rock. The conversation gets very dynamic and it's inspiring to hear students talk about their personal journeys and family histories. We tend to forget this right now, but most Americans came to this country as immigrants, and the stories of travel and western migration are still a huge part of the subconscious soul of America. They resonate deeply.

**SPRR: Anders, your bio says you're a creative writing fellow at the NEA. How is that going?**

**Anders:** There's no way I could praise the NEA loudly enough, or overstress its impact. The NEA has given me exactly what I—and all artists—need: the time and means to work. As a writer, it's the best thing that's ever happened to me. And considering the amount of artistic development the endowment has provided, the NEA will have its mark on everything I ever write. That's how monolithic the gift is.

**SPRR: We all have an interest in trains and railways. For me, there's something about their inherent meld of absence and distance, a sense that arrivals and departures echo off themselves. In Germany, I'd walk for hours along abandoned rail spurs. But your reactions are obviously more visceral. I love how you speak of attempting "to find beauty in the real-time happenings of life." As such, your poems are grounded in gut-level things, like those that ground the poetry of Philip Levine, Larry Levis, Richard Hugo, and Joe Millar. With such concrete images in mind, do abstractions ever attempt to creep into your poetry, those things Pound said we should vehemently beat back?**

**Anders:** I'm no good at thinking in abstraction. I think spatially. I think in story, image, and voice. When I was little I loved to draw. I drew images of bird's nests, dragons, and my favorite basketball players. I drew blueprints for imagined homes, marking the length of walls, the widths of doors. I also loved mimicking how people spoke, embodying another's words and delivery, getting the timing right. I loved listening to a good story, regardless of how many times I'd heard it before (still do). And Kai and I loved coming up with games, often attributing supernatural powers to sticks, doorknobs, swing sets, and trees. In other games we became animals or soldiers, always with some kind of backstory. Many years later, when I wrote my first poems for a poetry class in college, my instinct was to create active scenes, focusing on imagery, compressed narrative, voice, and encounters between characters. My very first poems were scenes with my mom at her church, and with my brother in our childhood backyard. My teachers at Fairhaven College (the best teachers I've ever had) helped me recognize the craft and content choices I was making, and helped me develop them. I've never used abstraction heavily, because it's just not the way I think. I don't start from concepts or themes; I start from stories and characters. I don't even start with language. I start with an impulse to tell a story, with music and images in my head, and that moves me to speak.

**Kai:** Trains have always been a minor obsession of mine. Ever since I was a kid I've been drawn to railroad tracks, abandoned freight yards, industrial landscapes, backcountry roads. Stuff like that. There's an obvious sadness to abandoned spaces, but there's also a humble dignity, and a sense of the *absence* of beauty. What's there is not exactly *what is*, but what once was and what might come again. The train is a symbol of this for me—the past and future connected by one long rail of galvanized steel. Anders and I grew up next to a railroad yard, so we could hear the trains at night when we went to bed. It was sort of a magic industrial playground, and I always associated the yard with a lost era in American history. When I write about trains now, I feel like I'm writing about a piece of my childhood. I feel like I'm exploring a personal space, but also a symbol that stretches beyond my upbringing in the Midwest, beyond the trains themselves and the weight of whatever they carried. I feel like I'm exploring a spiritual realm, in a sense. I'm a big fan of nouns and objects in poems, but I don't think there's anything inherently *wrong* with words like *fate* and *distance* and *spirit* and *love* and *soul*. It's just about how those words are handled. In Rilke's Letters to a Young Poet he says writers should use "the things that surround you," which is good advice, but then he goes on to write the Duino Elegies and Sonnets to Orpheus, which are so full of abstraction they're almost made of air. There are better ways and worse ways to write about this stuff, but I don't think there are wrong ways. I think the real danger is believing there are rules.

**SPRR: Kai, you went on in your *Poetry Northwest* interview to say that you want your lines "to paint a picture, to allow the reader to actively form an imaginative landscape." For us as editors, over-descriptive writing is often a reason we turn away submissions. When teaching or just speaking to others about writing, how do you address issues of economy of language?**

**Kai:** I think it's a matter of letting the reader into the poem, of letting them participate. When you create a potent description in a poem you are giving the reader an actual experience, something to remember. There's a way for them to access the poem and construct impressions internally. There's a huge difference between a poem that reflects the world and a poem that imagines the world as it *could be*. I'm interested in poems that allow the reader to construct a schema through associative distance, or *leaps* as Robert Bly calls them. When you create a leap, you create contrast, but you also create space. There is a web of feeling you begin to develop, but it doesn't come from the poem, it comes from the reader, from the mind of the reader as they piece things together. When you write poems that are urgent poems, focused on experience and feeling, I think the language naturally whittles itself down. Sometimes it works in the opposite way, where the feeling requires an excess of language, but again, I don't think this is a bad thing. I mean, how do you economize Whitman or Levis? They need those words and those lush descriptions for the poems to gather momentum. If you look at Roethke's great poem, *The Far Field*, which is one of my all-time favorite poems, it develops a whole road trip of experiences and descriptive tangents, but it creates such incredible power by the end: *A ripple widening from a single stone / Winding around the waters of the world.* Long or short, I want the poems I write to create an internal landscape for the reader. I think the biggest gift you can give a reader is insight, something they recognize for the first time in themselves. This only happens if they allow the poem inside, if you give them a way to make it their own.

**SPRR: Poetry is often stated to be the art of compression and suggestion, learning not what to say while letting silence do its own kind of speaking. When you write, does focus on these elements come naturally, in the first writing, or do they come later, during revision?**

**Kai:** I'm the kind of poet who writes ten poems and saves one, instead of writing one poem and editing it ten different times. I'll save the good ones, set them aside, and then slowly edit them for years before I show them to anyone or send them out for publication. The bulk of the poem, if it's going to be a good one, usually comes in the first or second draft. I work very hard writing poems, but I rely on inspiration to get me the good stuff. My process is sort of like finding cool rocks and dropping them in a river. I let time smooth the edges, but what appealed to me about the poem to begin with is still there. What I'm looking for is a kind of inherent energy, a uniqueness, and a way the poem creates a world beyond language. We've already mentioned Richard Hugo; he talks about this kind of thing in *The Triggering Town* where he suggests you need objective distance from a subject in order to create more invention and imaginative space. Sometimes this involves negative capability and suggestive textures, sometimes sound and silence, contrast in various elements of form, but I think it's nearly impossible to control this stuff. I think poetry can be taught to an extent, and I think we can isolate things when we talk about craft, but if I'm totally honest, I rarely think about any of this when I write. If I get something good it's partly a matter of instinct partly a matter of chance.

**SPRR: Do you both have full-length books or chapbooks on the horizon?**

**Anders:** We just launched our new co-chapbook, *Two-Headed Boy*, with Organic Weapon Arts. It's exciting to have this one out in the world, because it was the first chapbook we put together, and it's all about brothers—lots of freight trains and travel, too, but the focus is on the enduring bonds of brotherhood, and of family. Jamaal May did a gorgeous job with the design and Tarfia Faizullah was a wonderful editor. I couldn't be happier with it! My first full-length is in the works.

**Kai:** My first full-length collection, RAIL, is forthcoming from BOA Editions in 2018. The book is about riding freight trains, Midwestern landscapes, brotherhood, grief, depression, and the spiritual significance of the American West. It's a book about survival and the will of the soul to endure. I've been working on this project for the last twelve years and I'm extremely honored and thrilled to be able to share it with the world. Nothing in my life has meant more to me than this.

**SPRR: In my own writing, most of my revision involves saying something in as few words as possible without sounding overly austere. I constantly consult the Synonym Finder. But very often the word I seek takes a redeye flight and arrives in my brain at 1:13 am. For you guys, is revision mostly that honing, finding that edge of concision?**

**Anders:** I tend to work on a draft until I can't think of what else to do with it, then I memorize it and take night-walks around my neighborhood reciting it to myself. I think about what I could add or expand, but—like you—much of my revision is refining and cutting. For example, as I'm reciting a poem, if I get stuck on a line over and over again—can't remember it or get tongue twisted—I know I need to revise that line, or a line nearby (like with the body, sometimes a symptom shows up at a distance from the problem's source). The other day I was sawing plywood in the garage for a new bookshelf and suddenly thought of a better line for a poem I'm working on. It was a funny line, and a bit crude, so I grinned and shook my head and wrote it down, then picked up the saw again.

**SPRR: Both of you speak of older generations of writers as formative in the backgrounds of your creative experience. In addition to some of those same writers, I keep going back to writers like Katherine Anne Porter and James Salter. Are there contemporary writers that provide the same power for you?**

**Anders:** I'd recommend checking out Edgar Kunz, Hieu Minh Nguyen, Danez Smith, Essy Stone, Will Brewer, Katie Condon, Sam Sax, Tiana Clark, Matthew Wimberly, and Leila Chatti.

**SPRR: For you, is the author of a poem always its speaker?**

**Anders:** No. I write a lot of persona poems and love getting lost in their voices, their needs, their personalities, their senses of humor. I can feel totally transported inside a speaker's mind and body, and I have no idea what they're going to say before they say it. I've always liked listening carefully to how people speak, then mimicking it, and imagining what they'd say on a range of topics. I've had super interesting conversations with other writers about this process, because I seem to work backwards with characters: Instead of imagining a character's interiority and based on that interiority deciding what they'd say, I hear what they say in my head and write it down, then I ask myself what that means about their interior life. Apparently lots of writers do it the other way around.

As for poems that are rooted in autobiography: No, I don't consider myself the speaker in those poems, either. Poems are imaginative spaces and readers can use them any way they want. That's one of the great gifts of art: It's not set in stone; rather, it's interactive and sensitive to suggestion and context. A poem becomes what the reader needs it to be in any given moment, and that flexibility is perhaps its greatest power.

**SPRR: Anders, we share an interest in Neanderthals. They fascinate me because they were also hominoid, and also because they vanished. We keep learning more and more about them, how they were so much smarter than science initially thought. Yet they remain mysterious. I think of your poem, 'The Muscles in Their Throats' as re-accessing the primal. What is it that attracts you to them?**

**Anders:** To begin with, Neanderthals are ALMOST us, but not quite, which makes them dangerous and haunting. This closeness is also why skateboarders hate rollerbladers with a vengeance, yet have no reaction to basketball players—basketball being a different enough activity to neutralize any potential threat. There are all these questions about what Neanderthals could or couldn't do. Could they speak? Could they make art? Could they understand symbolism? Did they have names? And there's great fear of their abilities, because if they could do something that we do, than that thing isn't unique to us. They're a mirror and a warped mirror, and both are trouble for our ideas of ourselves.

Next, Neanderthals have suffered terrible speciesism, which has grown from—and been used to reinforce—the racism of some scientists studying them. For example, the prominent Neanderthal brow-ridge was once thought to be the result of a lifetime of furrowing the brow in a constant state of discomfort and anger. Neanderthals were also compared to the "savages of Africa," as proof that Africans were "undeveloped" humans. Over and over again, Neanderthals have been carved into narrative weapons, and used to tell stories that are designed to lift up certain groups of humans (Europeans/whites) and degrade all other humans. Every few years the story changes, and humans reimagine Neanderthals all over again. The current stories are much more hopeful and inclusive, celebrating cultural and biological differences, and are also rooted in more "accurate" science, although even "pure" science works from stories and preconceptions. It's simultaneously fascinating and terrifying. The study of Neanderthals becomes less about Neanderthals, and more a reflection of humans—our hopes, our fears, our desires, our corruption.

I'm also drawn to the process of paleontology, which involves dividing the earth into "squares" (one meter by one meter), then slowly digging down, one square at a time, carefully dusting for fossils and bones. And later, using tiny fossils and bones to build stories and whole imagined worlds. A finger bone can be our only evidence of an entire culture, which might have lasted for 400,000 years, and we're left to extrapolate from there, filling in everything else. It's much like poetry: a few carefully chosen lines are all we have, and those select words are forever surrounded by the silences and shadows they seem to create, the ghosts they conjure, the stories they hint at.

**SPRR: Richard Hugo said that it was better to write of the same things the same way than to fail at being innovative. Do you find yourselves writing of the same things, and if so, how do you keep it fresh?**

**Anders:** To me, Hugo's statement is misleading. Writing the same things repeatedly is not at odds with innovation; in fact, the two work well together. I think it's deeply valuable (and inevitable) to write of the same things, in the same ways, over and over again. Partly because once you have an idea or concept or topic, you need to flesh it out and give it a body so it can walk around. You can't do that quickly, or with only one poem. Even if one poem ends up being the pinnacle of years' worth of labor, and all the other, similar poems go unread, the labor was still part of the larger process that created the possibility and context for that one poem to be conceived. Through this process, you're also leaving behind a roadmap for future writers to study and learn from, and since weaker poems often show their seams more clearly, studying a poet's less effective pieces can be illuminating. But you're also constantly building on what you already know, and have already written, and this building through repetition is a good route toward innovation. I think circling back to the same obsessions again and again is often more fruitful than consciously abandoning your obsessions, for at least two reasons: 1) because our obsessions hold so much potency (and therefore potential) for us; it's where our energy resides, whether we like it or not. And 2) because—like with an individual story or poem—recycling content and coming full circle demands a complex type of innovation: you're covering old ground, and therefore you must find ways to make it fresh all over again. To put it another way, returning to the same material can often create better conditions for meaningful innovation, because you need to find a way to make the old new again, and you must do so within the restraints of history and tradition and

20

nostalgia. Whereas, innovation that wholly abandons old models is refusing to reckon with the weight and complexity of history, and often ends up being innovative—yes—but without real meaning.

**SPRR:  When I get stuck some place along the line when writing a poem — a difficulty finding the right word, or stuck on how to transcribe an image from my mind to the page — I get away from the poem and do something the opposite of writing, like physical work, or a long walk. It seems the creative part of my mind needs that break. Does that happen to you as well?**

**Anders:** Yeah, definitely. My college was an experimental interdisciplinary school and I designed my own degree called *Writing Through the Body*. My study was mostly creative writing, but the other part was studying the creative process. I took lots of classes in somatic psychology and focused on the body's role in creativity. I spent a whole semester writing in a range of physical states, and basically found that the more I exercised, the more I breathed deeply, and the more I remained physically flexible, the better I could think and therefore the better I could write. Not just in terms of better thought, but also range of thought, spontaneity of thought, and leaps in thought. I also found that I could conjure more humor if I was feeling awake physically. None of this was scientific, just subjective experience. But it seems to help me. I've also found that writing immediately after physical activity works wonders. I think this is because the body stills but the mind keeps racing forward, churning to help you navigate the next moment, the next peril. But with the external world becalmed, the electricity turns inward, the mental gears start to turn, and slowly, you begin to hear the music.

On the other hand, I wrote my best poem of the semester on a whim, in an anxious mood, and on a computer instead of handwritten. So I'd add that creativity seems to benefit from both setting up good patterns, and then shattering those patterns when the mood strikes.

**Kai:** Most definitely. I think this is one of the hardest parts about being a poet. Not necessarily the writing itself, but the traps your brain can fall into. You can easily get bored, distracted, annoyed by small things, you can start parodying yourself or ripping off the work of other writers. This is a serious problem and when you talk to other poets, you notice there's always a conversation about keeping yourself inspired. Poets tend to get anxious because they can waste whole days, whole hours doing nothing. Sometimes the poems get stuck in one place, spinning over and over themselves. Sometimes they don't come at all and you can actually listen to the sandgrains of your life softly tinking off the glass. It can get very lonely and depressing at times and it's good to have other things to do. When I was younger I was a semi-professional rollerblader. I would skate for hours every day, doing tricks and moving my body in ways that allowed my mind to roam free. It's hard to explain, but when you're engaging in dangerous physical activities your brain starts reacting in interesting ways to dopamine and adrenaline. Sounds become cleaner and images pull themselves more distinctively into relief. When I ride trains it's the same thing. Even when I bike around town or go for walks, my mind gets a little bit looser, willing to roam, and the words shake free.

**SPRR: I've found myself feeling a little silly at times standing around in a place few if any frequent — a shuttered cannery or factory, a field of rusted trucks and farm equipment, a long closed auto plant in Detroit — and a little voice in my head intrudes to try and tell me how absurd I am weaving a little**

**fiction in my head, looking to turn nowhere into somewhere in a poem, as it were. Anything akin to that ever come to you?**

**Anders:** Well, Kai and I are from fairly small towns in Minnesota––Northfield when we were little and Moorhead during our teen years. It's what we come from, and I think we've both maintained an affinity for, and interest in, rural culture. Most of the important moments of my life have happened in small towns, in the wilderness, or in abandoned buildings. While Kai and I were growing up, our family would drive out west to a camp in the Cascade Mountains called Holden Village. Holden used to be a copper mine, and, until recently, all the old structures were just sitting in Railroad Creek Valley, rusting for 50 years. There was a massive mill built on a sheer slope, stretching hundreds of feet up the mountainside, and the uppermost tailing pile above the mill was called the Third Level. Orange earth. Broken windows. Rocks ghosted with white viscous skins not unlike cauls where the creek from the mineshaft trickled. Stacks of doors. Piles of plumbing. Old snowmobiles. Rows upon rows of school buses. Styrofoam blocks as large as cars. Buildings filled with corroded antique junk, rusted treasures. We used to build obstacle courses, scavenge for rusted bolts to trade each other, shatter stacks of plate glass with a single brain-size rock. The orange earth lifting into dust devils and spinning down valley and dissolving. The Third Level was our playground. Over the years we made two films up there, played basketball on the court made out of a collapsed building's still-smooth cement floor, almost flooded the camp by damning the creek at the water treatment plant, and "skied" the 500-foot orange tailing pile in nothing but tennis shoes, generating an orange avalanche in our wake, breathing in clouds of orange dust, and what we didn't inhale caked our open wounds. That place is strong in my imagination, although now the whole mine is gone. It was dismantled one truckload at a time, bulldozed over, and the detritus

23

was loaded onto barges and ferried down valley. As a writer, I want to give voice to the places I've traveled, the towns I'm from, and the lands where I formed my mind and heart, and, even more so, I want to give voice to the people of those places—especially when they're no longer with us.

**Kai:** Totally. I understand that feeling. Anders and I grew up rollerblading together and one of my favorite things about skate culture was the variety of landscapes you find yourself in: run-down buildings, back alleys, abandoned warehouses, drainage ditches in the middle of nowhere. Just the most random parking lots and suburban strip malls you can imagine. Most people go about their day walking through these territories without seeing any value. They see them as wasted urban spaces or nondescript architecture that only serves a practical purpose. But when you're skater, you see a potential for the way you could skate these places. You see a visual potential for the way a certain trick could be photographed, or the way it might look in relation to a video. I think writers can develop a similar eye for imagining narrative potential, and I think it can extend beyond the scope of the writing itself. We already talked about railroad landscapes, but I think the absence of narrative or beauty can inspire a need for creation. Going back to skating, when we used to go to skateparks, it was always a fun time, but it was extremely boring compared to street skating. At a skatepark everything was laid out for you, designed to be perfect. Street skating was subversive, and usually involved some banal urban landscape never meant to be skated. It was an act of rebellious imagination to skate street. You had to *unsee* your surroundings in order to make it work. When I write about soy fields in Northern Minnesota, I don't do it because I think it's beautiful, or meaningful. I do it because I see an absence of beauty

24

**SPRR:** I often write poems set in places I've only traveled to on Google street maps or Wikipedia. I find myself viewing tons of internet pages on anything from wolf repopulation programs to the job descriptions of switchmen and longshoremen, all for a few facts that may be given context in a poem. You both strike me as those who write solely out of actual lived experiences. Is this always true for you?

**Anders:** I often start with personal experience, but like you, I do a ton of research for my poems. Research is one of my favorite parts of being a writer because it helps me take interest in a huge range of topics I otherwise ignore. For example, I don't know anything about guns or hunting, but I'm currently working on a piece about a hunter, so now I want to know everything about guns and hunting: the types of licenses and permits, the seasons, the types of guns, the types of game, the cleaning solutions, the gear, the scopes, the bullets—not to mention the lingo, the clothing styles, etc. And that's just one topic. For that same poem, I've also been researching taxidermy, the "caping" of deer for a shoulder mount, the anatomical differences between bucks and does, the history of Wounded Knee, the history of South Dakota, and the etymology of the words: deer, buck, lady, genuine, gender, and Cinderella.

I do research for almost all my poems, sometimes reading for hours to find one critical word. Even when a poem is deeply personal, there's always something in it that I don't know about: the term for a type of swivel lamp, a grain of wood, a type of baseball bat, the behavior of earthworms during a storm....Research is a way to go more deeply into your own writing, a way to fall more in love with the world.

**SPRR:** Related to the question above, I have a poem about my father shooting squirrels out of his English walnut trees. That's insane, of course, but the poem required it. In reality, my dad just said he might take his .22 rifle and shoot squirrels that had been eating his fruit trees. Bruce Weigl speaks of finding that juncture of memory and imagination that creates the poem. Hugo says the only truth in poetry is the truth of our feelings, our imagination. How vital is it for you that the poem be true to actual circumstances, or does what the poem demands evolve and show itself as the draft unfolds.

**Anders:** Poetry works on people's imaginations in a funny way, because it's fiction but people take it to be true—as in factual. It's not. Even when it is, it's not. (Neither is nonfiction, but that's another conversation.) Poetry isn't about the writer; it's about the reader and what they make of it, how they manipulate it, interpret it, expand it, etc. The facts of actual circumstances have nothing to do with it, even when they do.

**Kai:** Poetry is an outlaw territory and I think poets should write whatever they want. If it's completely made up, fine. If it stretches the truth, fine. If it imagines the world through persona, fine. I think the evolution and development of language and human culture requires this. But I'll admit, I do have a personal code for myself about what I can or can't write. It's not that I worry about the truth of an experience, so much as my relationship to an audience. Basically, at the end of the day, it's essential for me to be able to stand up in front of an audience and *believe* my own language. There's so much poetry that sounds fake to me. Uninspired. Imitative. Trendy. Pointless. It's not so much about staying close to reality, although that has something to do with it, but I think it does have to do with conviction and integrity. If I'm going to spend three years working on a poem, the poem needs to be about something larger than myself. It needs to be written to *connect* with another human being, and to allow them to connect with something in themselves. For me, the responsibility of this connection is huge, and it's important that an audience knows I'm bringing the language from the most honest place I can, from the depths of my heart, the fabric of my life. I want them to know this when they hear me read a poem. I want to be able to stand behind my words and say, *Yes, of all things, this is who I am, this is what I know.*

**SPRR: Would you consider yourselves "regionalists"? I mean that in a good way, where the poem is about specific locales, yet has something to say beyond any insular community or region.**

**Kai:** I sort of consider myself a metaphysical regionalist. I write a lot about the Midwest, about the West Coast, about specific places and people in those zones, but the important thing for me is the movement itself from spot to spot, voice to voice, poem to poem. In most of my poems place is a psychological state, as much as a physical one, and the significant thing is the motion in between. I think the reason for this is that growing up in the Midwest, and especially in Fargo, the impulse was always to leave. There was nothing at all on the horizon. No mountains, no trees. Just flat. You had a feeling of being everywhere and nowhere at once, of being in a place that was sort of a non-place. When I started reading Bly and Wright and Hugo, I recognized all the landscapes they wrote about—the farms, rivers, small towns, etc.—but I didn't recognize the feeling I'm talking about. I'm definitely working on place-based poetry, but it's complicated. The poems never want to take root. I've talked about this in other interviews before, but I should mention this story because it's related. When I was about nineteen years old I had a vision while I was watching a giant colony of ants. I was sitting on a hill in Southern California—sun going down—and I was watching all these ants on a treestump. They were running all over the place and my brain sort of tweaked out and I started seeing all these green lines running from one living thing to the next. It was this green, fluid, continuous web, and I was able to see and hear things from miles away. I know it sounds crazy, but it's a significant piece of my poetry, and it affected the way I write about place. I'm not so interested in the place I am, in the land itself. I'm more interested in the place I left behind, the speed I'm traveling, the place I'm hoping to go.

**SPRR:** Many writers elide political poems, or are disdainful of them altogether. I was in a class with Joe Millar and he told one classmate that if you write a political poem you've got two strikes against you because the reader already knows where you're going. I agree. Seems that when writing politically, the poet is so anxious to get a social or political point across that they trounce any pretense to art. They become Elmer Fudd trying to shoot Bugs Bunny, but all they do is blow away their garden while the rabbit escapes. How do you feel about that?

**Kai:** Haha, that rascally rabbit. I know what you mean about political poetry, but I think it's hard to avoid right now. Almost every conversation I have with poets these days involves political poetry in one form or another. Talk of politics, talk of identity. I think a lot of poets who don't write overtly political poems end up feeling isolated, or out of style. With everything going on in politics right now, all the obvious horrors we're facing with Donald Trump in office, who wants to read my poem about hitchhiking? Who wants to read my poems about depression? What do they matter? I think about this a lot. But even though I rarely write poems with political agendas, that doesn't necessarily mean my poems don't mean anything politically, or couldn't be viewed through a political lens. Sometimes writing about the Badlands in South Dakota is a kind of political stance. I mean, whether we like it or not, we inherit the cultural climate in which we live. We internalize these issues, react to them, even subconsciously. I think there are pitfalls in political poems just like any other type of poem, but one of poetry's great strengths is its ability to crystallize communal emotions. You see this in elegies, wedding poems, war poems, ballads. There's a long history and utility there. Political poetry might be the hot ticket right now, and it might seem the only thing anyone's paying attention to, but I don't think it should be actively avoided. We need poetry in politics a lot more than we need politics in politics. We need poems with a strong internal compass a lot more than we need to worry about pitfalls of craft. A poem that starts with a predetermined purpose isn't necessarily a bad thing. If a poem fails it fails due to a lack of imagination, not because it was written in a certain form or mode.

**SPRR: Do I detect in the poetry of you both that you rarely use figurative language, few or no similes or metaphors? If so, is it because you prefer to let the narrative itself become figurative?**

**Anders:** The amount of figurative language I use depends on the poem's subject and speaker. It's true that many of my poems use little or no simile or metaphor, and yes, that's often because the poem as a whole is working as a metaphor. But as I mentioned earlier, I often minimize figurative language when writing scenes of survival. In those cases, the formal choices (such as literal, minimalist language) are matching the content (literal narrative circumstance and basic human need).

In contrast, I also write a lot of persona poems, in which the focus is on voice and character, and figurative language is doled out like Halloween candy. So I'd say—in terms of language usage—I write in multiple modes, depending on what the poem demands.

**Kai:** This maybe goes back to the idea of documentary, but a lot of my poems are written in a space of experience. They begin in the moment, they wander a little, and they end in the moment again. I like this style of poem, and I've been writing it since I was young. don't know if I actively avoid figurative language, but I think I distrust it when I'm writing about real experience. It's a little like street photography, which I've been doing a lot lately. When you're walking around a city looking for strange combinations of things, for something to catch your eye, you don't have much time to think of a metaphor. You go on instinct. You *intuit* metaphoric potential as it happens. Sometimes it's only a fraction of a second, and you barely have time to understand why you looked at *that* person at *that* particular moment. You might not be fully aware of the meaning, but you still understand a *feeling* of contrast, of significance. I think the images and descriptions in my poems wor off a similar kind of instinct. Everything I write is symbolic. Everything is a metaphor. I just don't want the metaphor to be aware of its own significance, I want it to develop naturally, almos by accident. I think the impulse for metaphor is such a deep human instinct the brain creates associations whether we intend them or not. We start naming things in the world— grass, fencepost, twelv gauge, brother, wind—and before we know it a connection forms. A narrative develops and we feel a metaphoric weight. I like it bes when the metaphors are unknown to themselves, but they're in the shot just the same.

**SPRR: Regarding poem endings, what things do you consider when wrapping up a poem?**

**Anders:** The final line is the most important line in a poem, but in my experience, great endings are discovered as you arrive at them- -not before. I have so many unfinished poems where everything is in place except an ending. If I can't find an ending, the poem neve works, and I end up abandoning it. Once in a while, on a lucky night, I'll be taking a walk or doing the dishes and I'll suddenly think of a way to end a poem I wrote months or years ago. It's as if some small machinery has been cranking away in your mind, and then finally and gracefully and all at once, some piston falls into place. That's a rare and deeply satisfying feeling.

**SPRR: Is there anything else you'd like to add?**

**Anders:** I'd like to thank you, Jeff, for this opportunity, and I'd like to thank everyone in the poetry world for all the forms of support and encouragement you've shown toward Kai and me as brothers, particularly Organic Weapon Arts for publishing *Two-Headed Boy*, Diode Editions for publishing *mercy songs*, Floodgate Poetry Series for publishing *Northern Corn*, and all the journals and websites that have featured our poetry film, RIDING THE HIGHLINE: *Poets & Writers*, *New England Review*, *Ninth Letter*, *The Missouri Review*, and *Poetry Northwest*. And thanks to all the readers and dreamers.

෧

## Night Paths

*Mark Fitzgerald*

From goodbye to hello, the night takes me
in cold November as before. I leave
a weary basement for half a moon—tame
vibes, maples and elms, a vast maze of streets—
meander down an alley just for fun.
Snazzy music blares through streaked windows.
I enter a loft packed with friends beyond
redemption. My cup is filled, the band plays
softer. *A toast to Rimbaud's restless heart.*
To him, to us. Forget wisdom. Forget
the fire escape out the backroom. My heart
is grateful and the night bears new velvet.
No worries. Only a warm revival.
Only the slow laughter of arrival.

## Crow's Feet

*Danny Earl Simmons*

I ain't never been nowhere, not really.
The grooves at the sides of my eyes
make it seem like I been around, seen
some things, know what's what. But
that just ain't the case. No, them lines
from a whole lot of staying-put pain,
from being all the time surrounded
by too much come and too much go,
mostly go. I guess sometimes life's
just stumbling right into where you
s'posed to be, which is, maybe, same
as always being just a little too scared.
Still, I don't know if I'd do things too
awfully different if I started all the way
back from scratch. I'm used to these old
crow's feet in the mirror. I like knowing
how they got there – and I'll tell you what,
it weren't from staring all day long at the sun.

## Sweetwater

*Jeff Whitney*

Give me a town where there is more than one way home,
empty pockets at the billiard hole, homing pigeons shot straight
out of the sky. Everyday one long, singular hope that the badness
doesn't get in. It gets in. The plump moon howls, Zeus-armed
kids melt a city of monarchs, one living woman's grave
next to her dead husband's that boasts, "I won." Tell me
we don't belong a little bit everywhere. How we bow to the dark
night looking at our water's reflection, little act, but everyone is
dying. How a mother becomes her child and waits like god
for the world to get better, ghost of a future self she can approach,
unzip, step inside. We can be wrong our whole lives and still
in some way, shoot it right. That if we're lucky we won't know
what's coming, while the dead, like foxes, stay inside.

# Dear Mom

*Adrian C. Louis*

My old body shuffles absently
through these cluttered rooms.
I'm older than you when you died.

Owl murmur weaves through
a shaky, dark wind tonight.
There is so much unsaid.

Your muted love was never
enough to fill jagged wounds,
turned now to lovely scars.

I am exiled to a frozen land,
but the winter sun lightens
my scars, rekindles my love

& I am a smiling child again.
This is no convenient copout
& not a classical suppression.

Dear Mom, the sun is afire
like the place I suspect we will
meet up at.  I love you still.

# Where I'm Coming From

*Sam Robertson*

Big sky and a horizon in every direction
made the land smaller, more manageable,
so that, when reminded, you knew your friends
would think of you momently. Across town
that sun torched their brows with the same mood,
and if they wanted to move, they drove their car
on the same roads, through shared intersections.
One bar centered five adjacent neighborhoods.

No one left for very long, was back around
before you knew he or she was gone. No one cared
so great the feeling of security. Offense taken
variously became the way to feel alive, well;
and the future, like the land, stretched flat, so that
within infinite space one repaired one's image:
you could always and forever make up ground.
The market imported everything from kumquats

to fresh lobster, but only on weekends,
and what would be the fun of it otherwise?
You risked unfortunate acquaintance there
or at the more mundane Albertson's, a risk
pleasant to take, until it materialized. Big
souls interacted with more modest ones,
and both were happy to continue their errands.
I, too, left town in mystery.

## What Did You Love about Your Town?

*Steven Huff*


I guess the tactile sweetness of things, what else can I call it,

the myrtle, the violets, a treacle of dirt,

sanguine worm in the fingers, & sure,

it was a good town we landed in

after we fled Buffalo. A hobo on the tracks

carrying a ragged suitcase waved to us boys,

walking the ties into the blue dusk

in his busted shoes. All our family's Depression glass

was broken by then & we ate off the more solid

& heavy Syracuse China. Then, oh God,

the amazing authority of snow

stripped the trees naked & humiliated—

the possibilities of torment are endless, as you will realize

though probably not right away. You want

to evolve but we're hard-wired to pick ourselves

out of a lineup: You point at the one with

the worm in his fingers or the real *homme sérieux*

with the suitcase, & for a long time you

reckon this choice is self-knowledge,

though you can also pick the end of your life first

& try to make up what came before,

why you loved it so, and what the hell it was all about.

## On the Train Through Texas

*Jason Irwin*

North of Trinity, rows of corn pass
like pages in a flip book.
Iron fences and cow barns,
a blur of two lane towns.

I study my reflection in the window,
the lines around my eyes,
my graying hair, the deep veins
in my hands: blue knots unraveling
like a long held breath.

Time passes and not much changes.
Our griefs are wounded birds
we coddle in cupped hands.

The sun sets, flooding the fields
with an altocumulus light,
and in the distance
a heron takes flight, rising above
a bog of dead trees, to a place unseen.

# A Vision of Absolute Truth

*Jose A. Alcantara*

Two Spanish horses, beneath a bridge,
have traced their tracks in the snow.
Looking down, I cannot see the horses,
only the tracks, and though the curved lines
look delicate enough to be from deer
I know they are from horses, Spanish horses,
but how I know this, I could not say,
for I have never seen the horses,
nor could I tell a Spanish horse
from a Dutch horse, and I highly doubt
that we are, in fact, in Spain, a country
I have never visited. And yet I know,
absolutely, the only way one can know,
that there are horses down there,
Spanish horses, on white snow, and a river,
covered in ice, flowing underneath.

# Close

*Susan G. Duncan*

You double-dared me—you
bolder, stronger, beloved

younger brother—
to the top of the trestle

spanning the forbidden tracks.
Hand over small hand

each on a laddered climb,
apart by the width of a freight car.  Then

apart by the length of a roaring
eternity—

until the caboose is past, -
and your grin appears, and –

and we are closer—will never be –
closer.

*Justin Hamm*, **Train, Central Missouri**

# Lodged in my Mind

*June Blumenson*

i
We boarded the train in the dark
the only landscape—
our reflections fogged
in the steam of our breath
against the cold
sleeper-car window traveling
as if in an earlier century
like pilgrims to God's country.

ii
When I woke the moon
had slipped
into the morning sky
had slipped like a lie
into conversations had slipped
into my bones
brittle as Dakota winter.

iii
I took my coffee in the club car
an aftertaste of seared
bison and beer from the night
before—journaled the obliterate
horizon, missing scenes,
voluminous omissions. I felt bizarrely
orphaned, as if the mountain
I carried inside me had so diminished
it hardly resembled a small hill.

iv

The train stopped at a concrete
platform somewhere between
the Blackfeet Reservation to the east
and the Flathead Reservation
to the west. The porter unloaded
our bags and jumped back
on the train faster than the time
it took to whistle.

v

Moonlight flooded the timberline
cedars and a tall fortress
of spruce. The only evidence of life
was tracks, perhaps a wolverine
or lynx—fossil country
where no dense areas of human
contingencies exist.

vi

We trudged a half mile in the snow
to a small country house to sleep
for the night. The immense
wilderness lodged in my mind.
When I woke fits of sunlight
illuminated crystals blowing like gold
dust from rooftops,
landing singular in trees.

## New Streets
*Scott Davidson*

I am grateful for the house
and nine square feet of stoop
allowing me to stand
nose to nose with this new climate –
rain slanting like dull rage –
and not have to back away.

Miles to the north, the man whose legs
no longer support him is casting
for change, pushing through crowds
in a grocery cart, wrapped and covered
in so many coats he could melt and no
one would know. Some days I steer

toward the edge of the sidewalk.
Some days I just look away. Others
I dig in my pocket for coins, making
them ready to drop in his hand without
looking up, as if to say I'm sorry
there's not more when there is.

## John Stink

*Seth Copeland*

Scarfed like a vagrant babushka, hiding
the scrofula burls that give his unkind
moniker, he sits on the porch of the
home he's never entered, puffing a cigar
to glow while two of his cur dogs grease
their black mouths over a raw steak.
Passers-by get the scowl, or, if walking
too close, a glob of brown spit. Smiles
are not so much saved as implied for
local boys, who come up through the
cheatgrass and starthistles looking for
a fishing companion, one who will aid
their path to manhood with a tin of live
worms and a generous chaw of tobacco,
regale them with tales of the little people
as they draw black bass from Bird Creek.

Evenings, they go home with sick stomachs,
and the white mothers of Pawhuska feel
assured in their prejudice. As the setting
sun lifts the claws of the hawthorns up,
he curls to sleep, dreams of waking in a
cousin's cellar, mistaken for dead in the
snowstorm's bedlam, throat of his horse
sprayed in the snow, all he owned split in
a barter pile, and his name, *Ho-Ta-Moie*,
his real name, cursed, assigned to a ghost.

# Elysium, Asylum, A Silence

*Philip Schaefer*


In the season between seasons when the cormorant
becomes more stormcloud than shore, an injection
of Morse, when cows posture in the wind's knife
like bowling balls in a field of echoes, when the mirror
you once knew becomes a glass portal to a new truth,
something to crawl through, I will be waiting
at the end of the world (which is the end of silver
& solstice & childbirth & injustice) with a blindfold
for you. It will smell like the neighborhood that grew
out of your palms. It will beat like the warm metal
chamber on the other end of a stethoscope. Two fingers
thinking on a desk. It will hold the names of every person
you ever touched, stitched in blue. With one hand
on your shoulder, one memory in my teeth, we will walk
until the lake's basement makes animals of our feet.
We will navigate black waters and hold neon yellow fish
like little galaxies. Every moon has its hollow heart
and every pulse writes its own dying language
and every scratch of Sanskrit is a different version of gravity
so when I tell you to jump I mean fall backwards
from the plane that brought you here. Give yourself
to the sky. At the end of the world (which is the end
of mass murder & maple syrup & golf & missing hymnal
pages) I want you to take a torch and traverse
the cave until its walls shrink into your skin. Until
that comma of light at the end of the tunnel becomes a pillow
you can cut through, a song you can finally endlessly listen to.

## New Year's Day on the Devisadero Trail

*Branwyn Holroyd*

Turn your feet and walk towards the mountain.
Slip your body into the pocket of light
between mountain and falling snow.
Ascend the crooked path, red earth
and stones will hold you to the ground.
Follow the curving trail to the wordless place.
Melt a warm heart line in the snow
so you will know the way home.

Tilt your ear to the earth and listen.
Draw a picture of a heart with extra chambers—
a dazzling maze of blood, light, and sky.
Tuck it in your jacket beside two faded dollar bills
your lover tucked there for safekeeping.
Fill your pockets with stones, desert sage,
animal bones you found on the trail.

Listen to the echo pounding inside.
Sing like the thin-faced coyote
you encountered in the dusk.
Startled into stillness, you both ran
like long-eared rabbits. On the path
paws punched the icy crust,
stamped prints like flowers in the snow.

You don't know if you're flying or falling
as you leap from stone to stone,
almost lose yourself on the twisted trail.
You know one day you won't return
but will lose yourself in a spiral of ice and air,
unable to distinguish the body's edge—
where you end, and everything else begins.

Last night you dreamed of wild horses and wind
in the valley. Full of wonder, you woke
ready to be seduced by the slant of late December sun.
Today it is cold, the New Year approaches.
It is not a day for leaving.

## To a Friend, with Gratitude

*for Tony*

*Pam Baggett*

You listened as I described last year's
mountain visit, how I moved from the road
a rain of acorns, buckeyes, scarlet magnolia seeds
smaller than a fingernail. I was so tender
from my separation, crazed, really, at marriage's end
I couldn't bear the thought of them crushed.
To you, I vowed this trip to walk closer
to sanity, to recognize each creature's fate
as its own—

          until I came upon the mother possum
split open from a car's hard blow, four infants
scattered around her, hairless and blind.
I did what you would do: found a stranger
who lent a shovel, plastic bags to keep blood
from my hands. I picked up the little ones thrashing
on hot asphalt, placed them in shaded grass
at road's edge, worked the blade beneath the mother,
a bellyful of babies still in her pouch, latched
to cooling teats. I laid them all together,
waited as her young pawed the air, slowly,
slower. For pity's sake, for sanity.

# Burn

*Lanette Cadle*

Before spring in the Flint Hills
comes the smell of burn-off, not the steady
chemical flame that smokes oil town skies
at night but that uncontrolled burn
rippling across grasslands that combusts
seeds, pops them right open so that green
can follow. The slow red line rolls
across hills, relentless, at times jumping
the highway. Stars hang heavy in the sky,
roped by strips of smoke.
It's not always night, but often it is,
maybe to see the leading edge of flames
easier, maybe for secrecy, since outsiders
who don't know it's coming don't like it
and raise a ruckus writing newspapers
about the dangers after they finish
their drive through Kansas on I-70 or I-35,
bound for the excitement of Colorado
or Oklahoma. By then, the hills are green
again, more so against the black earth,
and cattle pour out the chute, lowing soft
at the clear sky, the milky stars.

## Invisible Stranger Route 2

*Michele Waering*

There is a reason fire blocks your view
and black smoke coils through your dream;
kerosene torches line the road, conspire,
send fire-reek into your face, flames
to snatch at your long white dream coat—
This is not your road anymore.

But if, when you waken,
you are still so determined,
find a street view skewed by years
and stand there—invisible stranger—
stare at the front porch, imagine
how much work it took to buttress
the east wall, raise the ground,
re-route the recalcitrant spring.

You can still hear summer aspens rustle
on the western side. Share whispers.
Ask them who tree-blocked the view
of Cherry Mountain from the road—
Young trees, years taller now:
click on them with your mind-fire—
your helpless arrow—

# Hassayampa River Preserve

*David E. Thomas*

A quiet place
       traffic sounds
              all around
big trees
narrow stream
of clear running water
             birds
and people looking
          at birds
vermillion flycatcher
       ladderback woodpecker
             cormorants
cottonwoods
leafed out
       still to bud
       up north
acres and acres
of saguaro cactus
       and greasewood
spread
either side
       of the highway.

d. thomas
28 February 2016
wickenburg az.

## Passing Through

*Byron Beynon*

A landscape of arthritic trees,

deformed skeletons and the bumpy,

unsealed road vibrating our frames.

The afternoon bakes,

powder-blue sky

clear and pure

as Sturt's Desert Pea

acts like a flame

in this wilderness.

Ant-hills the colour of rust,

tricks of light,

stand like gravestones,

black and green trees,

cattle, wind-vanes, telegraph poles,

the abandoned cars

all reel-by as we arrive at Camooweal.

No fuel for two hundred miles

as the sun sits on the horizon.

It is like entering a world of science fiction.

Soon, moonlight will lay a sword of silver

across this antique land.

Hushed and new as darkness comes

the smouldering day ends,

flaring bold again with opal stars.

## Highland Retreat

*Frank Light*

The wind relays a dialect, guttural, strange.
An irregular regiment debouches out its veins,
Disperses at dawn.
Fog, smoke, sun.

In the afternoon twin engines drone,
A mote from above or below,
The lay of the land,
River with footbridge, ribbon of sand,
Hills, hollows, huts, clothes on lines,
Trees, not all with leaves, ravines, vines,
Trails to paths, shrubs to grass,
Green to umber,
Slash.
Murmurs.

Farmers, hunters, dinner in a bowl.
High, low, vertigo,
Runway to and from afar.
Dirt to dust devils, anything's possible
Except the highway: clearly impassable.
Purpose leaves scars.
Scars rewind.
The old in a bind.
Youth so inclined.
Out with the plane.
All that remains.

# Byway

*Larry D. Thomas*

Safekeeper
of the quiet
of untrodden paths,

it's the sanctuary
of chariness
and whispered voices.

Anonymity
sidles up to its dive bar,
waits patiently

for a pint of beer
it never has to order,
and perks its ears

for intimations
of loss only it
can decipher.

The shadows
are its honored
guests, lengthening

so discreetly
nary a soul
ever notices.

# Back Roads

*Shaun Asbury*

In Kansas they take you
to farmlands fit for postcards

as proof you struggled well
through the past. But I bet,

at multiple points, you drifted
over center, slapping your face

like a cow's tail at a herd
of flies to handle the rolling

waist-high grass mile
after plain mile & nothing

unordinary to stake
the durations between

grain trucks. Not much more
will come if you forget Colorado

& head south instead
toward Wichita, which

will spring up like a mirage
& just as mythical as scenic views.

In fact, I hope you forgot Kansas,
clicked your heels & you're flying

fast over that crow's nest.
Though if you stopped

to stretch, if the gauge warned
you'd be stuck as a tractor

tire sprouting flowers if you didn't,
you could find yourself hypnotized

by mailboxes as mile markers.
You could be flailing in your city

of choice to forge a similar silence,
unsatisfied with this nowhere

now that you're here.

# Highway 99

*(for Celeste)*
*Karen G. Berry*


Downtown is miles behind me. I drive my country,
that long stretch of 99 that carries me to the suburbs,
where we pretend to keep it clean, but the dirt filters in,
the occasional adult bookstore, waterbed motel,
lingerie modeling studio, sneaking past the censors of suburbia.
It makes me laugh. I admire the rot. I drive it, my strip, my
highway.

I am driving too fast. I have on my RayBans.
My radio is too loud. I wore too much eye makeup today.
I am feeling kind of frisky in my forest green minivan
easing in an out of the lanes, cutting off the Cherokees,
living on the edge with no turn signals, needing
an oil change. I am one risky mama.

I pass the strip malls, Seven Elevens, Fabricland,
the organ store, so many goddamned coffee shops
because we are sleepy in this state,
the used baby boutiques, the spy store
for those hurting husbands and grieving wives
who want the evidence on film of a truth
held in a heart like cancer. I pass it by.

I roll past the Union Gospel Mission thriftshop
which has leased space to a yakisoba shop
and the reader board says "Jesus Rules Teriyaki"
I feel no call for God's heavenly yakisoba,
but who knows? Anything can happen
even gustatorial salvation. I drive on,
not tempted by the Burger King, Hot'n'Now,
McDonald's, or least of all Carls Junior.

I pass Kaddy's Cafe, where for fourteen years
I have made a mental note to stop for coffee
and never have. I drive by again, make that mental note
one more time. The band plays on.
I pass the retirement villas and the fruit stands
the bright and beautiful collision of concrete consumerism
with gentle hills and sleepy farms.

I soar down this highway on wings leased
month to month, while the music of
angry young women with multi-million dollar
recording contracts fills my velour and vinyl cockpit.
My voice rises in angry accompaniment,
as if it had anything at all to do with me anymore.

Through Tualatin, and Sherwood,
home of Robin Hood Days, never been,
and over Parret Mountain, which is no
mountain at all to a girl from Montana.
I climb up and swing down, riding
the deep, aching roll of descent.
Oh Pacific Highway, you own my soul.

I drove this road every day ten years ago,
my youngest baby asleep, her soft curls
and hot pink cheeks, her full mouth slack,
drops of drool precious as pearls to me,
an angel in the car seat while Peter Gabriel sang
the one song that always made me cry.
It was safe to cry while she slept and I drove
and he sang the song that will always take me back
to divorce, to betrayal, to pain so great
only her presence kept me from going over the bridge.

And it is like falling, after all, to reach the little town
I remember, here, at the place where this road forks
and I must choose to follow or not. Still here, still here,
we are all still here. I could continue. I could go south,
to points further, Dundee, beyond, following the trajectory
of my continuous automotive flight, arcing, soaring,
free until I reach the grey water that roars like
blood in the ears, but is cold enough to kill.
This town is where I stop. I only go this far.

## Search For Life On The Ohio River

*Andy Roberts*

I abandon the checkbook in disgust,
head out in the Honda, all windows open
in the death of December,
hotheaded, teary-eyed, hit ninety
to find something approaching peace of mind.
Slow down, look around.
One thousand men eating mashed potatoes,
all up and down the Ohio River,
losing teeth, one at a time.

I take the road north and discover
music at an empty rest stop,
melodies established with three notes.
These from small brown birds
who suffer terribly in the cold,
but hang on with numb feet to the wire
and continue singing.

Up and down the river I search
for life and find it
in the plainest places.
A killer sugar pie recipe
from a pregnant grandmother at Rooster's.
A one-armed mechanic in Marietta
who welds tight my cracked exhaust manifold
as I wait in his tin-roofed garage close to the kerosene heater.
A junkie at an NA meeting
who shows me how to
crush my oxy beneath a dollar bill,
roll the single for a straw.

I make my way back
to the checkbook, of course.
Practical, always practical.
Nose, a dollar bill dusted
with the fine residue of oxy.
Couple of loose teeth.

## It's August Again

*S.J. Dunning and Ciara Shuttleworth*


The tar sticks to your tires, Jeff, as you blast
ninety miles per hour toward the next home (foreclosed)
you've been dispatched to service. Road Warrior,


your daughter calls you. She says
you have driven to the moon
and part way back by now,
in the routine of yellow lines and fire-


scorched sagebrush. It's August again—
the month of your birth—a word that means
regal, exalted, monumental: none of which you feel
you will ever be (except in your daughter's eyes).
The miles before are the same


as those ahead, no place
to call *home*. But here—what stretches between—
holds you as you cross desert, remembering water
you used to manage, the "town ditch," a river's imitation,
a life ago. Once the god of so much,


you wander now, jerry-rigging
drive shaft, radiator, your failing teeth if you could.
*Stay in one place when you're lost* you used to say.
But what does destination matter
on these ribbons of asphalt you know better

than the motel bed where you'll sleep tonight,
your window cracked to siphon smoke
from your cigarette, otherwise lifeless air circulating
you and Gabriel, messenger of the gods in dog form,
your sole companion? If it wasn't for gravity,

you would be an astronaut the way you drift,
weightless, from one vacancy to the next, each
a desolation, an atmosphere, a pressure
you enter without a mask,
as if there could be no wasteland
you can't endure. So you're just out there, Jeff,

thirsty, and solitude is nothing you mind,
your tires orbiting. You are Earth-bound,
hatched from the late summer sky.

                              *


Kate of scorched landscape and sunflowers down
the hill, you reckon with potholed roads as you do
endless laundry and dishes, cooking three meals a day,
feeding everyone you love, and even those you don't—
we're all hungry. Escape is the closet where you've secreted
a bottle of Tullamore Dew, the Irish Wolfhound sniffing
at your bedroom door, as if soliciting a sip
of his heritage, as if you were the keeper of such things,
even for the animals, even for the old man who sleeps
without snoring in his studio below.
Can he hear you? You know

you drift through his dreams like the huge tumbleweeds
that catch the wheel-wells passing by on your dirt road—
as if they'll get somewhere new this time.
They won't. You know this. You stand before the sink,
one foot resting just above your knee, a stationary
pirouette, remembering the stage, choreography
you've saved from California coasts, tides,
childhood, through your Nebraska years when you taught
your daughters to dance, one in her poodle-dog tutu,
Dolly Parton spinning "Love is Like a Butterfly"
on the turntable. Out the window, the sun sets red
from the ruins of so many fires. It's August. Everything
is burning. And you, Kate, with your ice-blue
eyes, sip whiskey, can see waves
where there is nothing but smoke.

*

We retrieve the remains
of the Tullamore Dew,
the bottle Kate didn't take
when she left us for high desert,
Washington, the shadow
of the toothy mountain range
where so little rain falls, everything
between burning. We toast

to Jeff's birthday, to a man,
who, seventy miles farther into the flames
than Kate's call—*home safe*—
has been hosing ramblers, wrangling
livestock (spooked & rearing)
into borrowed trailers
since the first hint of smoky sky.
In a kitchen in Idaho,

we are neither saints nor heroines
as sun sets, as we revel at the myths that sustain us:
a mother bent over open oven, testing another roast,
a father returning to the road.

The dregs of our predecessors
rage down our throats
while we rest against the sink, thinking
of them, out there, trying
to be who they believe we need them to be.

## Through the Gap
*Chad Burrall*

god damn the interstates I told
brother Jim – I am in a place
called Letterkenny Township

and it does not connect to any
freeway – paradise left behind
rain gutters run down spouts

stretched over yards sidewalked
out to cinder slush pile streets
melt driven through a town where

cold clouds fell down foothills –
they wouldn't climb the mountain
again – could not pass the calico

who lay ribs down on the road –
who built this blacktop straight
up a mountain?  no switchbacks

up through always moving mists
where Bear Valley drinks down
rain to feed trees the snow steam –

show me how rocks crack how
boulders break around here –
road signs around here just say

don't litter better hunt safe
ain't no winter maintenance –
on my lonesome here now buddy,

highlands have not grown up
to be soft here in Upper Horse
Valley and I am the only damn

fool out running these roads
up where what's below is only
a use map laid out in a long

trough now tamed by the turnpike
down below where Conodeguinet
is fed by her many dark mouths.

## Return to the Country

*Robert Fillman*


Along Chestnut Hill Road
      wild daffodils sprout
      between old tires.
I would lie down
      in the long grass
      by the brown discarded mattress
but there's a trash fire burning
      in a rusty drum not far
      from my old tool shed.
The black smoke
      dumbs the photograph
      of my wife and I laughing
beside the chicken wire,
      hammer still in her hand,
      the field pushing behind us.
How it's all gone wrong
      even now in the cool
      hush of evening.
Our first summer
      in this house,
      we painted the trim
a robin's egg blue.
      The gate swung
      wildly on its hinges in a rain.
The wood floors creaked.
      All the nailheads and spackle,
      the putty on the windowsill—
and I think of the nerve it would take
      to walk the path
      to a stranger's door.

# Quartz

*Kersten Christianson*

With my fingertips I read
this chunk of amethyst.
From its story spills
a time-capsuled
house:  a calendar
page from 1995:  splash
of vodka, mummified cat
in the basement, tea
leaves, signs
of mice.

Outside, the moose
cow beds down,
flattens tall grasses
in lavender light.

The stone's jagged peaks
sporting alpenglow
red dive into kamikaze
free falls, the handwritten
script of what remains.

# Two Portraits of Hunger, South Carolina

*Ken Meisel*

On a lonesome stretch
of South Carolina

back country,
surrounded

by cotton,
yellow-eyed grass

and bees,
I see the girl

approaching me
down her

front porch
like she's a ghost

in white, threadbare
hand-me-downs.

She's carrying
a baby

in her skinny arms
like it's

a life-size
salamander.

She gazes at me
with lunatic eyes,

a sanitarium's
glaze,

cracks open
a smile

like it's
a mud snake

winding all
around me.

What is hunger
if we refuse

to face it,
face-to-face?

A boy circles
a lonesome party store

on a bicycle.
Does one-wheelers.

Spits his gum out.
Maybe he's ten –

skin, black
as a hard-shelled

mud turtle,
eyes green

as a largemouth bass,
river birch arms

waving leaf-hands
at me,

like he's in the wind.
He lights up a smoke.

Calls out to me –
do I have any extra

soda pop bottles,
to sell.

# chernobyl, downstream

*Mickey Cesar*


Behold towels, sand, cigarettes
a book, a beer, a tea. I have set
our picnic. The sun on the Dnieper
is wordless, here slightly interrupted
before the Black Sea. The cats have overrun
the café, Laika shouts at play. The day
warms, then cools, then reverts. Nothing
I might want to say translates, and
silence is not an option. The smoke
of the river cruise hangs low above the boat.


The crackers stay uneaten. The scent of shashlik
teases.


Summer lay before us like an endless sandbar
untrammeled, undisturbed. May fifth –
the sun slips, and I wonder on how many beaches
this vignette is repeated, by how many
old men alone.

**Secrets**

for WS Merwin

*Laurie Byro*


A pile of windfall apples becomes
a fox lying nose in tail, a sentinel for memory,
as the late sun turns its fur into rusty barbed wire.

We've traveled for days. I've told you before
about these mountain roads. About the man

who lived in a shack who borrowed water,
fried me a plate of catfish for my Halloween
treat. I called him Uncle Charley, but he wasn't

any relation of mine. The night we got caught swimming,
there was another who wore a hood, leafy and torn,

who watched with particular interest while I wrung
out my undershirt, scrubbed my skin pink before we
sat down to supper and I was forced to eat what

was good enough for them. What I thought I had left,
I kept finding again. A pile of hoods in our attic left

behind by the man and bleached white as bones. Clippings
of the pineys and the baby who had been stolen.
We find a fox lying nose to tail, a sentinel for memory,

sun glinting its fur rusty and I tell you, with lips bruised
like wind fall apples, I can't stay here. Me with my old

coat mended so neatly where I had sewn secrets into its
pockets. Me in my little girl's voice who tells
you a story with lips that are only slightly torn.

# Panama Memories 1955

*A.D. Winans*

the young Panamanian girl
sitting alongside her sister
dressed only in panties and bra
reading a comic book
and chewing on bubble gum
at a brothel called The Teenage Club
waiting for the first GI's to arrive

six girls lined-up like bowling pins
rooted to the long wooden bench
with zombie like stares doing
a woman's thing inside
a child's body.

## Undocumented

*Terry Ofner*

A night crossing.
Whispers among the arroyos.

Missing already the weight
of baby sister on my hip.

## Resolve

*Kersten Christianson*

That the hot flush of fireweed
would flare crimson on the frozen cheek
of winter, illuminate the bare, knock-

around birch branch into silence and court
its fine greenery again in summer.
That I could learn to live under a sky

not boasting of rain, taste the willow-
grazed flesh of moose.  That I could age
in this wild among bloom and harvest.

### *Un Beso*

*Mark Smith-Soto*

The woman waving good-by at my barred
window is not a woman, I see that now—
she's a kid, just a teenager, round faced
and frizzy haired, Flora her name, who hated

to leave me without stopping for a last *adiós*
at the barred window.  Will I ever love anyone
the way I loved her?  She knew it and loved
me back but swelled big around the middle so

was being packed home to Guanacaste
(I know now but didn't then) to a hovel there,
back when I was six and never thought the world
could exist without Flora in the morning

and Flora in the evening.  I wondered
why she was outside in the night waving
at me through the barred window.  She
must have put a box or piled some bricks

on the ground, she must have worked hard,
I know now, to peer in like that, and I was
wearing white pajamas scribbled all over
with baby *elefantes* in blue and red when

my name at the open window woke me up
and I stood on the bed and looked out
through the dark bars and there was Flora—
had she been crying a minute ago?— maybe,

but now she smiled and blew me *un besito*—
or no, wait, wasn't it that she somehow managed
to raise herself against the window, to rise
way up on tiptoe to give me a buss on the lips

right through the bars, the first kiss I ever got
that really mattered, a kiss that's half a dream,
the pressure of her lips on my lips, the sigh of
good-by, that pale, barred face fading to night.

# Like a Cradle with a Broken Rocker

*Pat Anthony*

It is after midnight as we lurch between ruts
on the dirt road twisting down from Chalma,
sanctuary for the Black Christ
to where the grandmother wanted to
go today on pilgrimage outside of Mexico City.

Grinding gears on the '56 Fairlane when it's not
stalled from overheating break the mountain silence
studded with campfires, the drifting strains
of countless guitars eddying with the wind.

We stop at a tiny cantina, stretch our legs
by the light of a flickering lantern, wind soughing
through my soaked skirt where the baby has wet me
through. Dozing now, bundled in her blue sweater
against more than this night's chill.

They pass around blue corn tortillas, rolling them
into cigarette tubes, sans crema. I nibble but have
no appetite except for a bed in the colonia, a distant ridge
of lights. Sip some cidral, settle in again, against that back
left door where the window crank digs into my side.

The grandmother tells her beads in barest of whispers
and I wonder for what she prays. Tomorrow she will take
her many years back to the hotel restaurant and bake
endless loaves of bolillo, perhaps a torta or two, turn out a flan.

By night she will come past to bid us goodnight
and go to her single bed in a corner of a tiny apartment where
another daughter raises twin girls and pays out endless thread,
doilies secret in their patterns as spiderwebs. I fight off sleep,
almost rocked now by this treacherous road, dozing off
with this baby girl who will grow up only to die before her cousin
who rides beneath the almost swell of my belly unseen.

## American Beauty
### *Matt McGee*

"Buy me a rose," Anna says.
We're drinking in a roadside bar no one likes
which is why we like it.
"Buy me a rose
and I'll show you something special.
Something...
American. "

The bent-spectacled Mexican
who trolls the bars and stands next to women
to guilt their dates into buying his $10 bouquets
wasn't far away, so I waved him in
plucked a rose from one of his pre-assembled
bunches and dropped $5 on the table,
more than enough for selling the next sucker
a rose-less bouquet.

Anna, in her too-short
bare navel cable-knit top
tilted her jeans down a little in front,
hiked the top dangerously high
and held the rose beside a laughingly
perfect belly button.

"Look familiar?"

I enjoyed the view
but no, it was lost on me.

"Didn't you ever see 'American Beauty?'"

Then it hit me:
I'd stumbled on that VHS case
during my Blockbuster days
and realized I was gazing at
the world's most famous bellybutton.

"They chose me for the shot," she says,
"because the actress wasn't available. So yeah,
I'm kinda someone's bellybutton double."

I ask if she makes residuals,
and when she says no,
I reach in my pocket
to finger the wad again
and make sure I can keep drinking
beside an American idol.

## 2nd Class Bus Station Oaxaca

*David E. Thomas*

Waiting room
benches along two walls
no Coke machine
a shrine to Our Lady
of The Sacred
Heart
"patrona de los desperadoes"
opposite
our bench
portrait
of Virgin and Child
wilting flowers
holy candle
burning
bottom
of its glass
a battered coin box
beneath
all this on concrete floor
a little dog
sleeps cool
morning heat
shimmers
the open door.

(for Al and Louise)

>       d. thomas
>       4 January 1978 (revised 7 Sept 2016)

## Crossing again, and again

*Kyle Moreno*

Cathedrals in Mexico used to remind
me of my grandmother – jagged cracks
on the outside and silence on the inside –

until she pulled me to her one warm
day along the foamy coast of Rosarito
Beach and told me she had slept with

my grandfather because of his 1967
Chevy Nova and his thick thick
mustache that curved toward his chin.

I was eleven then. Didn't understand the
philosophy behind having one too many
beers. Couldn't understand why she

was glassy-eyed and redder than usual.
All I knew was this new word she had
put into my mouth like a piece of smooth

chocolate: *Sexo. Sexo.* I asked my mother
what it meant but, widening her eyes and
pulling the drinks from grandmother, she

dismissed it. Besides the way the seagulls
cried and the fat pink shrimp I had for lunch
that day, I remember that my grandmother

said something about how everyone has an
animal inside them. That her husband was,
had been, a tiger. That he had made her a

woman. I know what this means now, and
because I know it has become a memory I
like to taste, in the back of my mind, just as

I would taste a bowl of beefy stew or the ear
of a gorgeous woman and it's why I keep
on crossing, again and again, into the land

of my grandmother. Into the land of my
grandfather.

Into myself.

# Crossing the 100<sup>th</sup> Meridian

*Robert Tremmel*

At Cozad, there are still
hoofmarks buried deep
behind the afternoon sun

shimmering haze, faint
contours of ridgelines
emerging in the distance

fading away

dried blood on the rocks along
Plum Creek, and the driest air
still to come.

## Leaving Amarillo

*Frank Reardon*

It wasn't long after my
my father used
one of his eleven
stolen credit cards
to pay for the hotel
when we hit Highway 40
and left Amarillo

Grizzly Tim,
three hundred pounds
of beer gut and beard,
fell asleep,
letting the full can of Schlitz
fall from his hand
and hit the back seat
floorboards

My nine year old fingers
ripped the lid off
a can of Van De Camp
beans,
and dunked the plastic
spoon into the can
and started to shovel
the uncooked beans
into my mouth

With bean juice running
down my face,
I wondered which credit card
my father used: Bill Winslow?
Justin Reynolds?
Ricky Betts?

I didn't question him,
never did. Sometimes,
and they were the best times,
I got to pretend I was the child
of one of the names
from the credit cards.

Like the time
I pretended to be Harry,
the mute and deaf son
of Jeff Dean, a banker
from Perryton.
For my performance
my dad let me choose
where we were going to eat.
I picked Pizza Hut.
It was always Pizza Hut.

He was an amazing man
back then. Full of confidence.
Thick black hair,
like midnight without stars.
An orange leather jacket,
and a crooked nose
that had been broken
in a fight back home

When we lived on the road
for his job, Grizzly Tim called him
"Frank",
I called him
whatever name was on
the credit card.

And when Grizzly Tim went to a bar,
my dad would buy donuts.
my face: all smiles and
powdered sugar,
we'd practice the con
in the new hotel

How to walk,
how to speak,
how to be silent,
and I'd perform it
to a fault

And he'd dust off an ashtray,
and hand it to me
like it was an award

"Speech, speech!"
He'd yell,
and I'd bow and thank
the audience:
the beds, the quilts,
the lamps, the light bulbs,
the television set
with rabbit ears,
and the Holy Bibles
never opened.

Tomorrow I'd be Larry Barnes,
son of Terrence Barnes,
oil man from Houston.
I'd get to have a limp,
the hotel owner
would call me "precious",
and my father would nod
and rub my red hair.

I didn't know it then
but I was his apprentice,
the accomplice
to many faceless lives
taken for a few hundred
each, but it didn't matter

I loved him,
still do,
even if I'm unsure
of who I am anymore.

# Crossing the County Border

*Ace Boggess*

lose yourself in a song on the radio
or the smell of a fast-

food burger in a bag
beside you in the passenger seat

where are those familiar streets
surrounding you like razor wire?

yesterday you were a man
buried to his neck in sand

yesterday you held the keys
to a car made out of stone.

## A Memory of Stone

*Cindy Huyser*

In the sun where traffic drones
a memory of her, six stones.

A prairie-eaten roof and scattered stone,
timbers gone to dust like hollow bone.

Six blocks tall and white as bone—
a memory of her, not far from home.

A memory of her. Beneath the sun
beneath the stones, a memory,

a gathering of bones. Beyond
the fence, the unmown grass,

the stones, a turning
as passing wheels slow.

# Get-Away Car, United States, 2017

*Naomi Shihab Nye*

Deep grooves of dust atop the books in our shelves.
Anyone else feel a constant need to apologize?
What happened in our nation? The only person
in our family who could translate is dead.

When I close my eyes, someone hopeful
cups a hand over a candle.  This shadow has no face.
Weather, soon to deteriorate - I love how people
say that. Right now we find little refuge inside a room.

Old Highway 90 heading west through Castroville…
a bakery offers square cheese pockets,
unsweet palm-sized delectable treats.
Maybe that's what we need.

Leaving the gray bulk of the city, ugly crush
of abandoned strip centers, sickening graffiti, happens
so quickly - a day's hand opens to release you.
Soon we will need to drive even farther,

to ruined towns like Langtry and Sanderson,
where the internet won't work to report
what our country has done.  Maybe there is a cave
no one lived in since the Kiowa tribes, with no writing

on any walls, no painted pictures of animals or flames,
just an ancient heap of ashes in one corner.
There were times we thought the stone ages
behind us.

## Wandering Away

*Lana Dean Highfill*

There's nothing that's stopping us – but us – from driving all the way o
until we can't see anymore. Nothing carved in stones, or maps
etched into our palms. So what is it keeping the key from turning,
setting blocks upon our path? It's light and shadow, tricks of our eyes,
a bend in the road. It's hard to read the signs through praying hands,
too far for U-turns, or erasures of tread in the sands.

## Errands

*Robert Ford*

When things were good and I still believed in us,
even the mundane obligations sang like whales,
and taking the wiry road down the hamstrings
of the island to its full-stop, on those bastard mornings,
a single cassette on the stereo to numb the losses,
always made unquestioned sense. Sometimes in
light hushed with pearls, sometimes with the blade
of the wind knifing clear to the marrow, I'd time each
arrival against the tide, sifting it for treasure, perform
the errands, light the fires. Then return to you, the road
now huddled into a spool of knees and elbows, the
mountain a tight wedge tripping over its own steps before
falling like a tantrum into the kettle-grey ocean below.

# To Hell with Horses

*Steven Huff*


To hell with horses. Though I feel second to them, graciously
muscled and arrogant. Whatever I do, a horse is always besting me.
My ex-wife rode them far and whinnying into the woods
and the fields beyond that and across some road off any map.
To hell with riding lessons, I'm always thrown and left in the gravel.
A coven of riders are pummeling over the hill even while
Mars landings and Jupiter probes fill the internet news in tech-logos.
But our old root imagination that once made us, and our horses and dog
is always under hoof. I mean, she's still on a roan
with thunder overhead, bounding up from a glacial valley
on an air current primal and frothing at its narrative of mane and loin,
forelock and flank. How in hell are we getting through
this life if we don't ride?  And some just can't. I'm sorry.

## Time and Tide

*Ann Howells*


Mist is silver stillness, a kind of quiet
you can't find in the city.
Objects appear charcoal sketches

on silk; it reflects my mood,
outsider looking in. Here,
in this local restaurant, two old men

sit in contemplation of breakfast.
It is not a morning for conversation.
A young woman in red sleeveless top

and jeans refills my coffee, silent as fog
at the window. Silver starfish in her ears,
rubber sandals on her feet, she looks

to be an islander: mud-colored eyes,
dark hair, staccato speech as if
her mouth is so infrequently used

that once open, words gush. I ask
where to rent a boat. She gazes
at the ceiling as if the answer will appear,

message in a magic 8-ball. *Jackie B*
*rents for parties, but if it's fishing*
*you want, folks fish right off*

*the bridge.* She gestures. *It's lit up nights,*
*and spot are biting real good.*
I contemplate the string-bound box

that rests on my floorboards. He was
always an island boy. Perhaps the bridge
will serve if I catch the tide just right.

## Traveling South by Train through Northern Florida in the 1950s

*Nancy Scott*

Swamp gas defines the character of bald cypress,
black gum, tangled Spanish moss suckled by decay,
and flesh-eating plants.

In a clearing the white egret poses in the sun.

Shackled zebra-men pound iron spikes in the opposite track,
securing our return
to the rhythm of wheat fields and morning glory.

## Quiescence

*Jill Dery*

Twenty-one floors up, dawn's
breaking on the hotel windows.
On my stomach, face slurred into
industrially laundered pillows. What
city is it this week? Doesn't matter. Am
anticipating the alarm—the local news.
The alarm comes from outside when
twenty waxwings smash into the windows.
On cue, like some demented cold war
drop drill, all fall down. I fumble for my
robe, take the stairs, check my cell, dying
for caffeine. Just outside the foyer twenty
dead and dying birds. Red drops seal spread
wings. No blood, all damage cleaves within.

## Your First Time at Ole's Big Game Steakhouse and Lounge

—Paxton, Nebraska

*Robert Tremmel*


To get here, think
east-west

the Platte, U.S.
30, I-80, parallel
sage-colored ridgelines
and the railroad, long
freights of hopper cars
and dark, sealed containers
with foreign graffiti
on the side, plowing
through silent cloud banks
of Angus, Simmental, Charolais

stock trucks in the street
outside, pick-ups, vans
with out-of-state tags, red
Camaro built for this space
with the top down

and inside, your server, flushed
from her afternoon
on the secret sandbar
and already bored
by tourists and cowboys

duck hunters with time
on their hands, kid
with the rubber Bowie knife

developers from Lincoln
fresh off the golf course
in pastel shirts, Dockers

tasseled loafers
without socks

and all of you, eating
in a fishbowl, glass eyes
glaring from the walls

pronghorn, elk, gazelle

kudu, impala, bull
elephant waving long
tapered tusks
over bloody ribeyes

and the polar bear
stepping down
off the snow
for another chat
behind the bar
with Marilyn Monroe.

## The Oracle at Amarillo

*Jay Udall*

Find the motel laundry room,
the one windowsill
smudged with ash and charred butts,
coffee stains and feedlot dust.

Listen through highway sighs,
gazing at the empty parking lot,
the fence shedding its brown paint,
and what's left of the sky.

All questions will be answered.

## Lone Star Desires at the Triple Six: A Pantoum Bent on Misbehaving

> *on the coastal plain near Corpus Christi—*
> *where Farm to Market Road 666 meets Farm to Market*
> *Road 1833*
>
> *David Meischen*

Did he wink in your direction? Sound him out, laughing.
Take a cue stick from the rack on the back wall. Chalk it.
Make small talk. Grin. You don't know a thing about
this roughneck at the bar. Deliberate: take a deep breath.

Too soon it's time to drain the dragon. Piss. Buy
a tall one for the roughneck as he turns to you laughing
at the sign behind the bar. *Lucifer drinks at the Triple Six.*
Make small talk. Grin. He doesn't know a thing about you.

Drain your longneck. Drop a greenback for another
and let your dragon tame a while, gun-shy
for now. Sag, slacken, slouch. Release will come.
A sign behind the bar: *Beer is but a moment's pleasure.*

Feel desire unfurl inside your tension.
Drain this Lone Star. Drop a greenback for another.
The stripes are yours. Smack one into the corner pocket.
Or not. Sag, slacken, slouch. Your turn will come again.

Light a Lucky Strike. Inhale and hold, release.
Watch the smoke unfurling like desire.
Bend and hold your gaze along the sight line:
the stripes are yours. Tap one into the corner pocket.

Swallow. Feel your center warming
as you light his cigarette from yours. Inhale and hold, release
your breath. Circle the table. Surrender:
turn and rest your gaze along the sight line.

One last longneck from the bar. Take a deep, deliberate
swallow. Feel yourself dissolving from the center.
Take your cue stick to the rack on the back wall. Rack it.
Let his words circle yours. Breathe in. And out. Surrender.

## That's Him

*Terry Ofner*


pulling his shadow
across the yard
like a sack of oats.

Here he is on the porch
selling his garden tools
to some strangers.

Nothing sad about that.

They left the engine running
so that they wouldn't
have to stay too long.

Money talks
but it is a dull dull
language.

The gravel in the driveway
snaps under the weight
as the car pulls away.

The supports are down.
The barn sags
in the rain.

## Loves Horses

*Ann Howells*

Two hours out of Memphis
Mari leans from the passenger-side door,
vomits on the graveled shoulder.
Her migraine hammers,
and the moving car intensifies it;
coffee we stopped for minutes ago
and swallowed pills
spatter dirt. We'll pause again
at the next truck stop,
but now she needs motion to cease,
gulps fresh air.
She's thinking forward to Knoxville,
how she'll lead horses to the barn,
lean into withers
as she removes bit and bridle,
brush sweaty flanks, offer apples
they'll accept between rubbery lips,
yellowed teeth.
She's loved horses since age five.

I've loved too. I taste Sam's lips,
want to lean into him
stroke sweaty flanks, but Mari
is not ready to reenter the car
though this unlighted highway
causes unease: its dips and curves,
its encroaching woods. Tractor trailers
fly past, occasional car with lone driver.
We pace the shoulder, gulp down air.

## Forgive Me

*Megan Merchant*

There was a wide
field and wind-spun
funnels

dipping to kiss
the land,

laying open
like a palm,

and the cows
huddled
in the pond,

cars sped past
while I read
an abbreviate version
of emergency procedures

to my husband
who dropped
every regret
into is foot
to burden the pedal
into *faster*.

I kept reading
to keep my knees
from
shaking
the seat
more than
the winds
batting
against
the frame,
and hold
the children
obliviously
safe.

It turns out
the underpass,
with it's steel & concrete
lumbering
was the last place
for refuge

something about
a vortex causing
suction that would
spit us out—

I was skimming.

Forgive me,
this poem
is crafted
after-the-fact

and as much
as I try

I cannot
press the smell
of wet grass
onto the white space,

or erect a brick
cabin
roadside
for the weary
or lost,

for those
outrunning

the land-shred,
and urge to calculate
wind-speed
as loss,

spitting us out
from the bridges
we built and
thought
would hold

enough to
tuck us safe.

# How Many Horizons Will Swallow Me Today?

*Ciara Shuttleworth*

Time zones and state lines,
yesterday's yesterday was a series of lush
southern forests, turkey vultures swinging heavy
above unseen carnage, and terrariums
of baby alligators at roadside fruit stands
peddling peaches and boiled peanuts.

Yesterday was unmemorable until I hit
the elm and box elder-lined fields
of Nebraska, all neatly sorted and cut
into fine squares, a mile from corner
to corner and a sky so blue I wanted to child-run
and fall among the furrows.

Today it's badlands and poverty, men
tucked-chin walking highway's edge, dusty
towns a small tornado could wipe clean. And tomorrow
horizons will be flecked with sand and salt,
flat stretches of 90 mph desert and scrub, a golden
sun setting on neon flickering to life in Reno.

## Down Near Pitkin's Farm

*Kevin Ridgeway*

we were lost, so we decided to get off
the road and drove into a clearing we
recognized from a previous beer bash
and inside the electric bath of the car's twin headlights
stood an enormous bull moose with antlers far
more brilliant than any art class attempt
at sculpture we'd seen, his funky brown asparagus
legs supporting a long torso that extended
high above our car, whose good brakes saved us from
having all of that beauty slaughter our awkwardness,
but it safely and nonchalantly wandered off into
the darkness while we hyperventilated and fogged
the windows with exclamations using words
that did not exist.

we pulled back onto the road in search of the small
campus inside whose dorms we hid from the winter
weather, our parents, the jazz ensemble concerts
and a surrounding wilderness with creatures
that were even stranger than us.

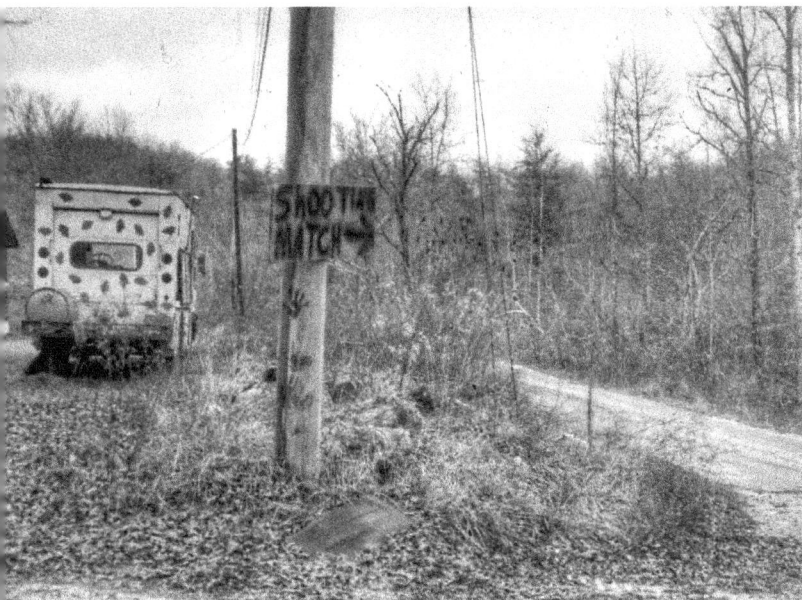

*Brett Taylor*, **Shooting Match**

## Sometimes rural America looks like crap

*Joe Cottonwood*

especially in sleet when you're driving
a vintage VW bus with a weak heater
north from Chesapeake Bay.
      It's all gray.
      The railroad tracks.
      The town with three bars and no cafe.
With my six-year-old son riding shotgun,
shivering, toweling the windshield,
I'm looking for some dead ancestor's homestead
but we'd settle for a warm drink and a cheeseburger.
      At a gas station we get heat-lamped hot dogs,
      a basket of backyard apples (tart and crunchy),
      their last pair of gloves
      (I wear the left, my son the right)
and directions down a dirt road
with cows plodding in front of us,
sloshing their udders
until a wet dog chases them away.

There's a structure missing half its wood siding.
Rock foundation.
While we're poking around, a red pickup stops.
A farm boy asks what we're doing.
He says somebody's stealing the weathered siding
        off that old outbuilding.
"Not me," I tell him, and we make to leave.
He tells me the land we're looking for is under water
        since they built the Conowingo Dam
        and we're in Pennsylvania now, anyway.
        There's no sign when you cross the line.


We pass a dead horse, vultures.
Farmhouses surrounded by trash and cars.
A hawk glaring from a bare tree.
To get home it'll be two hours by freeway
at the mercy of tractor-trailers
through the tunnel under Baltimore Harbor.
        "Sorry," I say to my son.
        "This is *great*," he says.
From me he got the explorer gene.
Icy road, we take it easy.
Somehow, a fine day.

## Crossed Roads

*Walter Bargen*

I'm not interested in back roads
as much as I'm interested in roads back.
Leaving this falling down century-old house
heated with chainsaws and the endless splitting
of logs, impossible to keep warm if you move more
than a couple feet away from the stove's glowing belly,
as if the wind walks freely from room to room.
The Volkswagen beetle's heater doesn't work,
no defrost. Backing out of the gravel driveway
easy enough, but heading down the icy hill is
a slow ballet sideways, backwards, then a full 360
before heading toward the snow-choked ditch,
stopping beside an oak.

To every season a turning yet the road doesn't
go on forever, but the meandering mortal list is long:
across the road a murder, suicide, wounding,
all in one night. South a quarter mile,
a friend wakes to the bright flare of sun
on the inside of his east wall, until he wonders at the time
and the sun rising in the west. He looks out the window,
the fire twisting the corrugated tin roof
into macabre shapes, leaving smolder and ash,
the blackened skull of an alcoholic.
The volunteer fire department declaring smoking in bed
and passing out.  A mile north, the police arrive
trailing a caterpillar plume of dust to arrest
the high school student making internet threats
against the local school.  The boy steps back
into the house, to grab a coat and hat,
and shoots himself.  Not a thought
to the road back or forward on a back road.

# Call me a bit slow, but...
### *Robert Ford*

it was almost exactly two of those
old-fashioned, pre-decimal years later,
on the other side of the world, and I was
nursing a rusted old dragon of a truck
down a red road you could see streaking by
through the lacy floor of the cab. And it was
just after midday, because the shadows
were mean and riveted on, and I don't
know why, but all of a sudden I realised
you'd actually meant what you'd said,
that they hadn't been just giddy, disposable,
2 a.m. words you might say to almost anyone
at all, to be laughed off the next day, like dust
from a mirror. It was possible that if I eased
further off the gas, I wouldn't get back until
everything was already picked and safely in
the chiller. And I wondered if those brahmans,
drawn and incongruously skeletal in such a
fleshy, civilised country, would be nosing
around in their paddock again, grazing on
fresh air, amazing me that they survived.

# McKruger's Place, 10:17 a.m., with Locust

*Laurie Klein*

Sweat and decline,

vinyl seats coughing up foam.

At Ray's Salvage

shucked-off suburban skins

molder, or rust, out loud.

Wire hangers jangle like egos

and rage clamps his jaw.
Even the locust, stunned
against the pickup's grille,

mimics corrosion: axles cocked,
pistons, implied. One wing
flutters, a small flag.

     Ray's woman
studies the tiny catapult legs,
draws closer, slow, slow,
to distance herself from

her old man's cracked heel

gunning the engine.

    A blue roar.

Belch from the tailpipe,

her whisper: *We're not dead yet.*
Flight, she thinks, is only
the down stroke's lift,
each upstroke stalling

the subsequent fall. Hope

crackles, its static eclipsed
by the horn, his shout: *Get in!*
And now she must leap
to reclaim the shape of a soul
defying everything used up between them.

## Outskirts

*Clarence Wolfshohl*

Do you know the outskirts?
That part of town delicately poised
between concrete and loam.
Not the suburbs with their planned streets
and houses alike in different ways.
But the outskirts, where houses poke
from the ground like random weeds
scattered along gravel roads
grown from cow paths.  Where vacant
fields wait under some speculator's thumb
or entice boys to wilderness adventure.

Do you know the outskirts?
Where stray cats collect
with interest, and bodies are found
face down in sumac brush.  The area
of junkyards with rusted 1950 Studebakers
and black mountains of rubber.  Where town kids
park on dead-end roads to drink beer or make love.

Do you know the outskirts?
Some flounced like taffeta hills
rolling ankle length from the city's edge,
and some short as miniskirts
high on the long legs of country roads,
only a brief delay before the city streets.

Do you know the outskirts?
Sandy and dry or boggy and wet.
Grey and weathered shacks or mobile homes.
A no-man's land out of all jurisdiction,
out of well-plotted time.
Where kids roam with restless abandon,
discover pockets they never can own.

## How the Hell Did I Get Here

*Ron Wallace*


How the hell did I get here,
here to this blue ending of summer?
When last I took my bearings
      and checked my compass,
I was bending curve balls around the corner of July
or chasing two grey eyes,
that laughed at me from beneath dark gypsy curls.


Now every time I pass a jukebox
      or turn on a radio,
I hear Willie Nelson singing
"Ain't It Funny How Time Slips Away".
None of these classic DJ's ever heard of J.J. Cale
"They Call Me the Breeze"?


One wrong turn,
coming out of Colorado,
blowing smoke to all four corners of the sky
      and a man winds up surrounded
by a pack of over-ripe evangelicals
beating Bibles into bayonets and breathing fire.


How the hell did I get here?
I swear I never saw that road sign
      never heard the warning horn,
just stepped out of the smoke and wreckage
and heard the siren's wail.

## Redwoods Diner

*Keli Osborn*

Hard to read the age of a stranger who calls everyone Honey. She
brings biscuits and gravy, Frisbee-sized pancakes, coffee black as
45s. She laughed, a snort, when asked for a soy latté. Her knee
brace is the color of dishwater and droops at the hinge. Her
shoulders sag inside a long T-shirt, her brows into parentheses.
There's a story behind her eyes—let's say hissing radiators and
rusted swing sets, stern stepfather who threw her out of the house,
the childhood sweetheart lost to a hunting accident. At a back
table, she joshes the regulars, delivers pork chops and hash
browns. Somebody wants more maple syrup. She limps toward
the kitchen, whistles a familiar tune. I want her to hum Hank
Williams. I want to wash her apron.

*Brett Taylor*, **Outhouse by a Church**

## Passenger

*Elizabeth W. Jackson*

Midnight roads glint with rain, throw me
curves as I drive towards the straightaway
back to our rented cabin.

*Do you think I should return that dress?*

Mom, I don't know.

*I love that pink color, but the sleeves,
they're just too short. They show too much arm.
What do you think?*

I shake my head remembering
those three hours in the Purple Chemise.

*Do we have enough coffee for tomorrow?
Maybe you can get some if we don't. I've got
to wash my hair in the morning.*

*Have you ever tried Pert shampoo? I just bought some.*

Our headlights skim trunks of hemlocks and pines,
whisking past their silence, and her head pivots
to stare out the back window.

*Did you see that man? I think he was limping.
Where do you think he's going?*

In the rearview, I see no one. The forest
leans over the road, everything black.

## Crossthreaded

*Jeff DeBellis*


The lugnut goes on crossthreaded again.
I crush my knuckles between the ground
and the tire iron trying to get it off.
I curse, kick the gravel. It's almost dark
but heat still shimmers in waves above the asphalt.

Ten p.m., Athens, Ohio.
Too late to cross the mountains.
Sitting at the bar and the blur
of topography and time
catches up. Three days on the road. Maybe four.
My body is heavy on the stool
and the tang of inertia runs all the way to my head.

I look at you and you know,
order for both of us. My head falls onto your shoulder
and stays there until the drinks come.
We never had a chance, but
we've always had this.

We're in the foothills now.
The rolling mounds that flank the Ohio
and mark the start of the Allegheny Plateau.
You rummage through your bag,
find a quarter for the meter. Fifteen more minutes.
Then we'll go.

# 29 miles

*W.P. Osborn*

. . . so left by the back way to follow ruts and holes that rocked and jounced
and squeaked the springs. And that motion after hours with the kivas, homes,
the silenced craft, religion, science, shale walls radiating trails where Pueblo
people and their animals dwelt and vanished, and maybe also the risk
we took in bringing off-pavement the Hertz we'd leased with 29 odometer
miles, got beneath my skeptic distancing. I'm not taking in the scenery much,
lurching, bouncing up and side to side in dust, trying not to slow-mo wreck
or stick us in a sage country no one would ever come and pull us out of.

By dirt and gravel road washing ruts through vacant land, big and curious
and wary and challenging, not bay nor the rock-red of sandstone geology—
shiny like ticket bait, with the sheen of blood—in a naked pasture a red horse
stood. It stood alert, hard-eyed as it would, ears up, nervous hooves,
as if it knew of a failure to journey deep enough into where I'd been that day,
and where I was. He reared low and spun and dipped his gleaming head
and stepped across the field away as if to have us come, but we were past him
then and with the progress we weren't making would not turn back or stop.
I didn't think of this as anything but another detail to take in in that country
—rincón, petroglyph, rock work, stallion—till later, when I connected
his appearance to the Canyon, the dwellers transient there a thousand years
before our passing through, our own red horse a tourist Ford sedan—
a world I never truly entered nor was equipped to comprehend.

# Bus

*D. Dina Friedman*


The seats were grey. We sat by the empties
waiting for prophets to appear—frowsy
ladies, men with stringy hair.

What messages could they convey?
It was so cliché—a joke not taken
seriously. We were two college girls

sleeping away opportunity. How many
miles to Milwaukee? Did it matter
when we arrived? Could we find ourselves

racking up cities passed through? Toward
the end, we didn't care, rolled
our bags, slept under the clouded sky

where you thought you saw a rattlesnake,
but we didn't consider the Bible, or original
sin. Had we missed some hidden symbolism

in the dimly lit stations? Had we learned
deprivation, our budget hotly defying
assumptions of what Americans should lust for?

Or, did we simply fall
into the whine of solid-lined highway,
bypassing all the exit signs.

## Antique Pain

*Gail Tyson*

Antique pain sneaks up on this country road
miles from our last fight, your name on a mailbox.

No one wants old lovers to settle down
in a rustic farmhouse, fig tree ripe

in front, sweet clouds of laundry out back,
domestic goddess stirring harmony
with a hand-carved spoon.

Back then, you couldn't wait to be gone,
preferring knife-edged dawn to my strangled

intimacies, never staying in one
place for very long, at least not mine.

No matter how far I've come with a man
whose goodness will take me a lifetime

to understand, this pain turns up, a letter
lost for years, skin-deep paper cut. I gun
the engine, drive away.

## Criminal Husk, Pulaski Heights

*Jesse Breite*

Ain't no blues like a West Markham midnight
streaked rubber-black.

Out of windows, young braves crawl into night,
gassing horse-power,
their bodies. The highway thrums.

Stoplights flash bluntly like diseased
constellations.
Fluorescent light bulbs in the rear view.

A girl lets her hair back through cracked windows.
I was there sucking thick air
with fat breath. Whiskey-fire glows heavy
in our blood.

Little Rock's roads bend and blacken,
stain-gross, like rummaged thighs.

Under the electric torch at Stifft Station,
we huddle fumbling for smokes.

Old men throw bags
into dumpsters. Flies anoint the bruised
flesh of liquored fruit.

On a late afternoon in Atlanta,
my wife eases the bad peach-flesh out
with a dull blade.
I eat what's left. The juice leaks
down my chin.

## The Hitchhiker

*David Armand*

My father was coming home.
It was three in the morning,
and he was driving down Hwy 47
in Chalmette, Louisiana.
This was after twelve long hours
of trawling for shrimp
in Lake Borgne and the bayous
surrounding it—returning
with his nets empty.

Then, in that early morning dark,
he saw a hunched-over old man
hitchhiking on side of the road.
My father slowed, then stopped,
and decided to pick him up.
After all, the man looked harmless,
not to mention it was cold.

The cracked domelight glowed
as the hitchhiker got in the cab,
and my father saw his dirty clothes,
long beard—the smell of him—
and thought he was doing
a good thing: until he pulled
off and the old man grabbed
a knife from his coat.

He held its rusty blade against
my father's throat, told him
to give over his wallet.
So my father leaned forward,
not saying a word, one hand
still on the steering wheel—
and reaching with the other
as if methodically going for
what the old man wanted.

But he grabbed a gun instead,
pushing its cold barrel
against the old man's head, knocking
away the knife, slamming the brakes
and forcing the hitchhiker out
before his truck even stopped.

And I still imagine that old man
on the cold gravel shoulder,
watching the red taillights
from my father's truck
diminish now into a single point,
astonished at his turn of bad luck
and wondering who in the hell.
had just picked him up.

# All I Could Think About That Summer

*Ricki Mandeville*

was leaving.
Driving west and south
toward an unbroken horizon.

I'd have nothing but country,
small town with a tired highway through,
two gas stations, a couple of cafes
where I'd eat at the counter and watch
one-syllable waitresses
slinging burgers and pie
to men in boots, men with dirt
in the creases of their shirts and foreheads.
Meringue melting in the heat,
collective drawl.
I'd rent a little clapboard house,
find a country FM station,
keep it on all night.
Be found by some stray dog
who'd decide to stay,
sleeping outside my back door
in the cool mornings.

I wanted midnight and passing trains,
dust and thunder, the threat of storm.
Flies zooming in through the screen door
before it banged shut.
The jelly mouth
of the neighbor's four-year-old, his face
pressed against my chain link fence.

But here I am in the bathroom mirror,
without a sleeping dog or kamikaze flies.
And somewhere beyond the concrete
there's a midnight train paused at a whistle stop,
an empty seat by a window.

# To Florida

*Jessica Jacobs*


In the citrus light of winter, I stole oranges
from your trees; through your white sand, tore
bike tracks ragged as rope burns. In you, I was a primal thing.
                                    For years,
I carried a keychain in your image, my name
stamped along its length.
                              We were always claiming you,
weren't we? Your every pine
                  a scarred tally of who loved whom
and when. But even before I could brush my own hair, I marched
into my parents' room and declared, *I'm not from here.*

By *here*,
of course, I meant you.
                              Though I'd never seen them, I dreamt
of mountains, of a landscape tall enough to hold me. So, yes, my first
betrayal of you was that early, that inconsolable.


        At Ponce De Leon's fountain, eternal youth
had an egg-rot stink. I wouldn't drink. All I wanted was to grow old enough
to leave you.
                  Florida, we never had a chance.
Empty buzzsaw of jet skis, creatures lurking the darkness
of our dock. And other darknesses, too:
The swak of girls' thighs leaving the seat of my car. All
the lipglossed mouths from which I couldn't look away.

Land of mowed lawns, state of near perpetual summer, in you
my longing knew no seasons. No dormancy. Eighteen years
was enough.


But my night mind grieves you. Now that I don't have to,
I come home often—for in my dreams
I just remember: swim and swim
through a day when sun columns your water
into a great hall, silt sifting like dust motes through the light; a hall
where all my earliest incarnations sit down to feast
while I skim that water's skin, calling
down to the ones I used to be.

## Alison

*Michael Dwayne Smith*


The smell of fresh-plucked lemon, braided
scent of citrus and grazing horses and the back
of your neck in mid-afternoon.

The impasto-green fruit tree leaves
sticking to every scene,
San Gabriel valley breeze a brushstroke
on the little brown curl of hair behind your ear.

The road in and the road out the same.

The northside train tracks in mud, dust in my hat.
The sleepy highway at grove's edge,
sometimes the orange summer foothills

on fire, sunset
whirling around the dirt path, you spinning
and spinning in that orange-blossom print dress

your mother sewed you, nimble, near dancing,
the valley flooding with calm,
my hands, tart fingers, my history and being,
the dry mouth of my future

all fallen out of fear, my heart unwashed.
The creaky wood house, straw-tinted at sunrise,
leaning slightly to the south,

my blanket melancholy for your heat,
for the shape of you,
me hungry for the pink grapefruit of your mouth.

The road in and the road out the same.

The once-sweet groves, like me, like the lake
nearby, have soured in drought,
but I do still spin at the thought of us, and every
highway, every fire, still runs to you.

# Birches

*Sasha Goodwin*

From the back of the cab
flipbook of trees and highway signs.
Then the dirt roads shaking the car loose.
A horse's breath when it lifts its head
and the aluminum mailboxes on tilted stems.
Everywhere bare branches as I near the house.

The gray pond beneath the heavens
holds swans whose tail-like necks
swing round to scan the verge for foxes.
Then plunge their heads into the bank
for roots, for beetles,
the greens that dangle from a dinosaur's jaws.

We turn into the driveway greeted by the old cape
with its thin and wavy windows, you're still here—
limping through the field toward the pond
to gather shoots for cattail soup.

**341**

*Tiffany Buck*

This heat can make you want to kill something.

That's what Baine tells his wife- a woman who ain't full here.

"You gonna kill something then?"

"If I get lucky…"

Baine looks at his gun locked in the cabinet. It's just too goddamn hot to hunt.

"Fulton, Duval, Glynn, Cobb, Douglas…"

"What are you doing, Annie?"

"Watching the out of towners go through the water on the road…"

"That ain't no water, it's a mirage; just happens in the heat."

"No, its water, me and Joey went playing in it yesterday, just past that old oak. Joey got soaked to the bone."

"Joey been dead a long time…"

"Just because you two disagree on football teams don't make him dead to you.

"Joey's funeral was thirty years ago."

The game was supposed to start in an hour, just enough time to kill something.

# Ways to Love a Back Road

*John Milkereit*

I love your back road but you're married.

The back road begins by loving you while standing in line for a ticket.

The back road washed away at Hotel ZaZa. You exited
     and therefore I love that one or both of us belong in a reality show.

I love the back road where you returned my Rolling Stones cassette tapes
     under my windshield wiper.

I love our back road fishing—
     how we caught nothing in our makeshift sailboat.

I love this back road until you make me crash.

I love the back road of your eyes.

I love that our back road up Stone Mountain was the Wrong Way.
     The helicopter lost us after we camouflaged with granite.

I love the back road that is running with you on Peachtree Road.
     I love our pain when we reach Heartbreak Hill at Piedmont Hospital.

I love the back road that is the Chattahoochee River. Beer is in the middle
     of our raft. This is parallel to College Initiation Byway.

I love the back road from Beaufort when we stole the soccer game
     and the homecoming cake. I love how my team was considered weak.

I love the back road you took with your cigarette and my green balloon
     on Saint Patrick's Day. I felt like a clown at a truck stop.

I love the disco taxicab driver that drove a back road
     to the Rammstein concert. I love that I could love Germany.

What I don't love about your back road is your eyes.

I don't love the back road when your heart is closed for winter.

147

## Where You Are

*M. Scott Douglass*

You are here
                    and here
          and here.
Every rest stop tries
to red-arrow you into place
on a piece of paper framed
behind glass to protect it
from bleary-eyed graffiti
and wayward steerage.

You were there
                    and there.
You remember going off-
road to stretch your legs, test
the local cuisine. Your waitress
migrated from Austin, bright
eyes, pretty smile, she forgot
you soon after your tip met
the bottom of her apron.

You are here
                    going there.
Your map is a jumble of rusty
road signs, scarred vehicles,
blurred landscapes, faces
in silhouette. You're a ghost
passing through the walls of lives
with no fixed destination,
but a tireless need to say
you've been somewhere.

# Highway 85

*David Chorlton*

A desert prison lies at rest
beneath sweeps of light
that break through changing clouds
on the day after rain
                    and wet
shadows cling to the rock
formations on the bright side
of the highway
                as sun picks out
remaining pools and vegetation
stripped to its winter core
                            on land
pulling free from a harrier's grip.

## A Lost Place

*William Virgil Davis*

Now no more than a trace of trail,
it had once been a road that only a few
knew. To find it you would need to
go beyond the last farm, the farthest
field, through a stand of thickened oak,
around the deep end of a small pond,
then up another hill, and beyond.

Once there, there wasn't much to do
except take in the view, then turn
around and come back to where
you started from, and belonged.

## Acknowledgments

Jason Irwin, "On the Train Through Texas," *A Blister of Stars* (Low Ghost Press, 2016).

Laurie Byro, "Secrets," *Redactions*.

Frank Light, "Highland Retreat," O-Dark-Thirty's *The Report, A journal of The Veteran's Writing Project*

Nancy Scott, "Traveling South by Train through Northern Florida in the 1950s,"

*Down to the Quick* (Plain View Press, 2007).

Mark Smith-Soto, "*Un Beso*," *Kakalak* (Main Street Rag Publishing, 2013). *Time Pieces*, (Main Street Rag Publishing, 2015).

## *In Memoriam*

Brigit Pegeen Kelly

1951 – 2016

You stand,
with those taken
   for all they're worth:

. . .

The way things fast
 toward their absent
    forms: go in hunger.

Go in grace.

— from *Field Song*

**Jose A. Alcantara** works in a bookstore in Aspen, Colorado. His poems have appeared, or are forthcoming, in *The American Journal of Poetry*, *Beloit Poetry Journal*, *The Midwest Quarterly*, *Spoon River Poetry Review*, & *Atticus Review*. Jose is a former Fishtrap Fellow and was the winner of the 2017 Patricia Bibby Memorial Scholarship from Tebot Bach.

**Pat Anthony** writes from the rural center of America, exploring roads at every opportunity and in all seasons, both for the experience as well as for inspiration.

**David Armand** was born and raised in Louisiana. He now teaches at Southeastern Louisiana University, where he also serves as associate editor for Louisiana Literature Press. He has published three novels, a memoir, and collection of poetry.

**Shaun Asbury** is a two-time graduate of Youngstown State University. His work has appeared in *Kestrel* and *San Pedro River Review*. A Kansas native, he currently calls Tucson, AZ home.

**Pam Baggett's** work appears or is forthcoming in *Atlanta Review, Crab Orchard Review, Greensboro Review, Kakalak, Nimrod,* and *Tar River Poetry*. Poems also appear in several anthologies, including *Forgetting Home: Poems About Alzheimers* and *The Southern Poetry Anthology Volume VII: North Carolina*. She is a 2017 recipient of the Ella Fountain Pratt Emerging Artists Grant and teaches free poetry workshops through her local library in Hillsborough, NC.

**Walter Bargen** has published 19 books of poetry. Recent books include: *Days Like This Are Necessary: New & Selected Poems* (2009) and *Trouble Behind Glass Doors* (2013), and *Too Quick for the Living* (2017). His awards include: a National Endowment for the Arts Fellowship and the William Rockhill Nelson Award. He was appointed the first poet laureate of Missouri (2008-2009). www.walterbargen.com

**Karen G. Berry** is a writer who lives and works in Portland, Oregon. Her poetry has appeared online in *Goblin Fruit, Prairie Poetry, Fireweed, Dream Journal, Napalm and Novocaine, Mothers Always Write, Ekphrastic Journal* and numerous print anthologies. She's the author of one novel and co-author of another. She gave up telling lies for telling stories in her early twenties and has never regretted the choice. She blogs at https://karengberry.mywriting.network/

154

**Byron Beynon** lives in Swansea, Wales. His work has appeared in several publications including San Pedro River Review, The Yellow Nib, London Magazine and Poetry Wales. Recent collections include The Echoing Coastline (Agenda Editions) and Through Ilston Wood (Lapwing Publications).

**June Blumenson** teaches poetry classes, curates a poetry reading series, reads her work at various venues in Minneapolis and is a member of The Minnesota Poetry Therapy Network, The Loft Literary Center and Banfill-Loche Center for the Arts. Her work has appeared in over a dozen books, magazines and literary journals including most recently *Comstock Review, San Pedro River Review, Literal Latte, Earth's Daughters* and the 2017 anthology *When Time and Space Conspire*. Her poetry manuscript *A Scythe of Moon* is currently looking for a home.

**Ace Boggess** is author of the novel *A Song Without a Melody* (Hyperborea Publishing, 2016) and two books of poetry, most recently, *The Prisoners* (Brick Road Poetry Press, 2014). Forthcoming is a third poetry collection: *Ultra-Deep Field* (Brick Road). His writing has appeared in *Harvard Review, Mid-American Review, RATTLE, River Styx, North Dakota Quarterly* and many other journals. He lives in Charleston, West Virginia.

**Jesse Breite's** recent poetry has appeared or is forthcoming in *Tar River Poetry, Crab Orchard Review, The Briar Cliff Review*, and *Prairie Schooner*. He has been featured in *Town Creek Poetry* and *The Southern Poetry Anthology, Volume V: Georgia. FutureCycle Press* published his first chapbook, *The Knife Collector*, in 2013.

**Tiffany Buck** is married with a spirited little girl. She lives in Georgia on the edge of Appalachia. She's lived in most parts of Georgia from the coast, to the mountains, and lastly metropolitan Atlanta.

**Chad Burrall** is a West Virginia native residing in the northern panhandle of that state. He is the author of *Allegheny Moments - Haiku and Photographs from the Appalachian Foothills*, has placed in the WV Writers Contest, and is currently working on his first full book of poetry. He is a graduate of West Virginia University and can be found as often as possible seeking inspiration from true characters, pool rooms, back roads, lonesome trails, and trout streams.

**Laurie Byro** has had three collections of poetry published, most recently *Wonder* (Little Lantern Press) and *Gertrude Stein's Salon and Other Legends* (Blue Horse Press) which contains work that received a New

Jersey Poetry Prize. Her poetry has received 49 Interboard Competition honors including 10 First Place awards as judged. In April 2017, she will receive her 2nd New Jersey Poet's Prize for a poem appearing in her forthcoming collection.

**Lanette Cadle** teaches rhetoric and creative writing at Missouri State University in Springfield, one state over from her home state of Kansas. She has previously published poetry in *TAB: The Journal of Poetry and Poetics*, *Yellow Chair Review*, *Rose Red Review*, *Stirring*, and *By&By Poetry*.

**Mickey Cesar** is an American English teacher who has lived in Kyiv, Ukraine, with his cat, Stasya, since completing his MFA in Creative Writing from the University of Kansas in 2011. He is the author of two full-length poetry collections, *Vanishing Point* (2005) and *If I Were On Fire* (Spartan Press, 2011).

**David Chorlton** is a 36-year resident of Arizona, having moved from the old world. He currently has poems as part of the "Fires of Change" exhibition at Tucson's U of A Art Museum, shown through March of this year. His book "A Field Guide to Fire" is his contribution to the project.

**Kersten Christianson** is a raven-watching, moon-gazing, high school English-teaching Alaskan. When not exploring the summer lands and dark winter of the Yukon Territory, she lives in Sitka, Alaska with her husband and photographer Bruce Christianson, and daughter Rie. She completed her MFA in Creative Writing/Poetry through the University of Alaska Anchorage (2016).

**Seth Copeland** is the founding editor of *Jazz Cigarette*, and a Publishing Editor for *The New Plains Review*. His poems have recently appeared in *pioneertown*, *This Land*, *Red River Review*, and *concis*, among others. He lives and studies in central Oklahoma.

**Joe Cottonwood** has worked as a carpenter, plumber, and electrician for most of his life. Nights, he writes. His most recent book is *99 Jobs: Blood, Sweat, and Houses*. joecottonwood.com

**Scott Davidson** lives with his wife in Missoula, MT, where he works for an organic soap manufacturer. He's received a Pushcart Prize nomination for poetry and a GE Young Writers Award nomination for literary essay His poems have appeared in *The Potomac Review*, *Poets/Painters/Composers*

*Blue Unicorn, Shadow Road Quarterly, Cirque*, and the Permanent Press anthology *Crossing the River: Poets of the Western United States*.

**William Virgil Davis's** most recent book of poetry is *Dismantlements of Silence: Poems Selected and New* (2015). He has published five other books of poetry: *The Bones Poems; Landscape and Journey*, which won the New Criterion Poetry Prize and the Helen C. Smith Memorial Award for Poetry; *Winter Light; The Dark Hours*, which won the Calliope Press Chapbook Prize; *One Way to Reconstruct the Scene*, which won the Yale Series of Younger Poets Prize. His poems have appeared in most of the major periodicals, here and abroad, including *Agenda, The Atlantic Monthly, The Gettysburg Review, The Georgia Review, The Harvard Review, The Hopkins Review, The Hudson Review, The Nation, The New Criterion, PN Review, Poetry, The Sewanee Review, Southwest Review, The Southern Review*, and *TriQuarterly*, among many others.

**Lana Dean Highfill** holds an MFA in Writing from Pacific University in Forest Grove, OR. She writes poetry in Southern Indiana, where she is an English professor. Her interests include live music, comic books, sci-fi, and marine biology. She has been published in *Three Drops Cauldron, Rose Red Review*, and *Nota Bene*, Phi Theta Kappa's honors anthology, and is currently working on her first manuscript.

**Jeff DeBellis'** recent poems and essays appear in *Appalachian Heritage, Gastronomica, The Wayfarer*, and *The Drake*, among others. He lives in the Appalachian Mountains with his dog, Pizza, and an unnamed cactus.

**Jill Dery** has published stories in *Bellingham Review, 13th Moon, Fourteen Hills*, and *The MacGuffin*. Her poem "Summer Solstice Anchorage" has been published in Autumn Issue 19, 2016, of *Antiphon*. She received an MFA in poetry from UC Irvine. Born and raised in Los Angeles, she's lived in Anchorage, AK, since 1992.

**M. Scott Douglass** grew up in Pittsburgh and lives in Charlotte, NC with his wife Jill. His poetry has appeared in places such as *The Asheville Poetry Review, Iodine Poetry Journal, Southern Poetry Review*, and *Sundog* and is forthcoming in *Gargoyle, North American Review, Midwest Review*, and *Slipstream*. His books include, *Auditioning for Heaven* (2001), *Balancing on Two Wheels* (2003), *Steel Womb Revisited* (2005), and *Hard to Love* (2012). He is a Pushcart Prize nominee and a NC Arts & Science Council grant recipient. His cover designs have won two PICA Awards and several Indie Press nominations.

**Susan G. Duncan** is presently a consultant with a performing and visual arts clientele, capping a long career in arts administration. She served as executive director for San Francisco's musical comedy phenomenon Beach Blanket Babylon, the *al fresco* California Shakespeare Theater, and the Grammy-winning, all-male vocal ensemble Chanticleer. Her work has appeared in *Atlanta Review, Blast Furnace, Compass Rose, the G.W. Review, The MacGuffin, OmniArts, Poem, River Oak Review,* and *Thema* among others.

**S.J. Dunning** lives in Tacoma, Washington. She is Co-Editor-in-Chief and Nonfiction Editor of *5x5 Literary Magazine* and teaches English online. Previous work of hers has appeared in *The Boiler, Front Porch Journal, Dogwood, Creative Nonfiction,* and other journals.

**Robert Fillman** won the poetry writing contest at the 2016 Pennsylvania Writers Conference. His poems have recently appeared in *The Chaffin Journal, Chiron Review, Glassworks, Off the Coast, Spillway, Third Wednesday,* and others. He is currently a Ph.D. candidate and Teaching Fellow at Lehigh University, where he also runs the Drown Writers Series. He lives in eastern Pennsylvania with his wife, Melissa, and their two children, Emma and Robbie.

**Mark Fitzgerald** is the author of *By Way of Dust and Rain,* which was published by Cinnamon Press and was a finalist for the Elixir Press Poetry Award. His poetry has appeared in numerous literary periodicals, including the *Santa Clara Review, Slipstream, Naugatuck River Review, Crab Creek Review,* and *Beltway Poetry Quarterly.* He teaches writing at the University of Maryland.

**Robert Ford** lives on the east coast of Scotland. His poetry has appeared in both print and online publications in the UK and US, including *Antiphon, Clear Poetry, Homestead Review* and *Ink, Sweat and Tears.* More of his work can be found at https://wezzlehead.wordpress.com/

**D. Dina Friedman** has received two Pushcart Prize nominations and published in many journals including *Calyx, Kentucky Review, Bloodroot, The Sun, Anderbo,* and *Rhino.* Dina is also the author of two young adult novels, She has an MFA from Lesley University and teaches at the University of Massachusetts/Amherst. http://www.ddinafriedman.com.

**Sasha Goodwin** lives in Seattle and will soon receive her MFA from Pacific University. She's been nominated for Best New Poets 2017. In her work she attempts to let everyday circumstances and objects represent what's unsaid in the piece. Her poems are informed by her childhood in Maine and love of the natural world for its fierceness and beauty.

**Justin Hamm** is the author of a full-length collection of poems, Lessons in Ruin, and two poetry chapbooks. His poetry has been awarded the Stanley Hanks Prize from the St. Louis Poetry Center and has appeared in *Nimrod*, *Sugar House Review*, *The Midwest Quarterly*, and *New Poetry from the Midwest*.

**Steven Huff** is the author of two books of poetry, most recently *More Daring Escapes* (2008), and a collection of stories, *A Pig in Paris* (2008). He is a Pushcart Prize winner in fiction and an O.Henry finalist. The Founding Publisher and Editor at Tiger Bark Press, he teaches creative writing at the Solstice Low-Residency MFA Program at Pine Manor College in Boston, and lives in Rochester, NY. He has edited a volume of essays, *Knowing Knott: Essays on an American Poet*, due out in February 2017.

**Cindy Huyser** is a poet and editor who lives in Austin, Texas. Her work has twice been nominated for the Pushcart Prize, and her most recent books are "Burning Number Five: Power Plant Poems" (Blue Horse Press, 2014) and, as editor with Scott Wiggerman, "Bearing the Mask: Southwestern Persona Poems" (Dos Gatos Press, 2016).

**Branwyn Holroyd** is from Vancouver, British Columbia, but she tends to wander. She currently passes much of her time in Oklahoma and northern New Mexico. She will graduate in January 2017 from the Red Earth MFA at Oklahoma City University. She has work published in the literary journal, *Cirque*, and in *POETS UNiTe! The LiTFUSE @10 Anthology*.

**Ann Howells's** poetry appears in *Borderlands*, *Spillway*, *THEMA* and elsewhere. She has edited *Illya's Honey* since 1999, recently going digital (www.IllyasHoney.com) and taking a co-editor. Her publications include: *Black Crow in Flight (*Main Street Rag), *Under a Lone Star* (Village Books Press), *Letters for My Daughter* (Flutter Press), and *Cattlemen & Cadillacs*, anthology of DFW poets she edited (Dallas Poets Community Press). Ann served as President of Dallas Poets Community, a 501-c-3, for four years and as Treasurer for many more. She has four times been nominated for a Pushcart.

**Cindy Huyser** is a poet and editor who lives in Austin, Texas. Her work has twice been nominated for the Pushcart Prize, and her most recent books are *Burning Number Five: Power Plant Poems* (Blue Horse Press, 2014) and, as editor with Scott Wiggerman, *Bearing the Mask: Southwestern Persona Poems* (Dos Gatos Press, 2016).

**Jason Irwin** is the author of *A Blister of Stars* (Low Ghost, 2016), *Watering the Dead* (Pavement Saw Press, 2008), winner of the Transcontinental Poetry Award, and the chapbooks *Where You Are* (Night Ballet Press, 2014), & *Some Days It's A Love Story* (Slipstream Press, 2005). He grew up in Dunkirk, NY, and now lives in Pittsburgh. www.jasonirwin.blogspot.com

**Elizabeth W. Jackson** is a practicing psychologist and writer with poems published in anthologies and literary magazines. These include *Crab Orchard Review, LUMINA, Poet Lore*, and *The Southern Poetry Anthology Volume VII: North Carolina*. In 2014, she won the James Applewhite Poetry Prize.

**Jessica Jacobs** is the author of *Pelvis with Distance*, winner of the New Mexico Book Award in Poetry and a finalist for the Lambda Literary Award. Her chapbook *In Whatever Light Left to Us* was published by Sibling Rivalry Press in 2016. An avid long-distance runner, Jessica has worked as a rock climbing instructor, bartender, and professor, and now serves as the Associate Editor of *Beloit Poetry Journal*. She lives in Asheville, North Carolina, with her wife, the poet Nickole Brown.

**Laurie Klein** is the author of *Where the Sky Opens*, and *Bodies of Water, Bodies of Flesh*. Her poems have appeared in *Barrow Street, The Southern Review, MAR, Terrain, New Letters*, and *Rivers of Earth and Sky: Poems for the Twenty-first Century. She blogs at lauriekleinscribe.com*

**Frank Light** has returned to the love of writing that led, many years ago, to an MFA in fiction from the University of California at Irvine. In recent years literary journals and anthologies have published a number of his poems and essays, many of the latter adapted from a draft memoir titled *Adjust to Dust: On The Backroads of Southern Afghanistan.*

**Adrian C. Louis's** latest book is *Random Exorcisms* (Pleiades Press, 2016). Widely anthologized and the author of a dozen books, his poems have been published in many literary magazines including *The Kenyon Review, Ploughshares, New Letters, North Dakota Quarterly, The Nation, Chicago Review, Prairie Schooner,* and *The North American Review.* He lives in Minnesota.

**Ricki Mandeville** is a freelance editor and two-time Pushcart Prize nominee whose poetry has appeared in previous issues of *San Pedro River Review*, as well as in *Gravel, Penumbra, Comstock Review, Galway Review*, and other publications, with new work forthcoming in Texas Poetry Calendar 2017. She lives and writes near the ocean in Huntington Beach, CA. She is the author of *A Thin Strand of Lights* and two chapbooks.

**Matt McGee** has traveled so much in recent years that he finally disconnected his cable and canceled his landline, afraid that hobos might start comfortably nesting in his absence. The road seems to have finally led back to his house, where he publishes *Falling Star Magazine*, an LA-based quarterly. His latest collection, *How I Learned to Love Joyce Carol Oates*, is on Amazon.

**David Meischen** recently won the 2017 Kay Cattarulla Award for Best Short Story. He has poems in *Borderlands, San Pedro River Review, Southern Poetry Review,* and elsewhere. A Pushcart nominee, he is co-founder of Dos Gatos Press, publisher of *Wingbeats* and *Wingbeats II*, collections of poetry writing exercises. His fiction and nonfiction have appeared in *The Gettysburg Review* and *Salamander,* among others.

**Ken Meisel** is a poet from the Detroit area, a 2012 Kresge Arts Literary Fellow, and a Pushcart Prize nominee with publications in *Rattle, San Pedro River Review, Boxcar Review, Midwest Gothic* and *Pirene's Fountain*. His books include *The Drunken Sweetheart at My Door* (FutureCycle Press: 2015), *Scrap Metal Mantra Poems* (Main Street Rag: 2013), and *Beautiful Rust* (Bottom Dog Press: 2009).

**Megan Merchant** is mostly forthcoming. She is the author of two full-length poetry collections: *Gravel Ghosts* (Glass Lyre Press, 2016 Book of the Year), *The Dark's Humming* (2015 Lyrebird Prize, Glass Lyre Press, forthcoming 2017), four chapbooks, and a children's book with Philomel Books. You can find her work at meganmerchant.wix.com/poet.

**John Milkereit** is a rotating equipment engineer working at an engineering contracting firm in Houston, TX. His poems have appeared in various literary journals including previous issues of *San Pedro River Review*. He recently completed a low-residency M.F.A. program in Creative Writing at the Rainier Writing Workshop in Tacoma, WA. His collection of poems, *A Rotating Equipment Engineer is Never Finished,* was published March 2015 (Ink Brush Press).

**Kyle Moreno** was born in 1986 and has lived in Northeast Los Angeles for most of his life. Although he has put up with an array of jobs, he has been heard saying that writing is the only kind of work that really, at the end of a hard day, pleases him.

**Terry Ofner** has published poetry in *World Order*, *100 Words*, *Ghazal Page*, *Flying Island* and *Eclectica*. He is an editor for an educational publishing company headquartered in Iowa, where he grew up—not far from the Mississippi River.

**Keli Osborn** writes and lives in Eugene, Oregon, where she co-coordinates Windfall, a reading series in its fourth decade, and works with community organizations. Her poems have appeared in *Timberline Review*, *The Fourth River*, *Elohi Gadugi Journal* and the anthologies, *The Absence of Something Specified* and *All We Can Hold*.

**W.P. Osborn's** *Seven Tales and Seven Stories* won the 2013 Unboxed Book Fiction Prize, selected by Francine Prose. He has short fiction in journals such as *Mississippi Review*, *Another Chicago Magazine*, *Cream City Review*, *Gargoyle*, and *Gettysburg Review*, and poetry in *Hotel Amerika*, *Main Street Rag*, and *Pinyon Review*. wposborn.com

**Frank Reardon** was born in 1974 in Boston, Massachusetts, and currently lives in Minot, North Dakota. Frank has published poetry and short stories in many reviews, journals and online zines. His first poetry collection, *Interstate Chokehold*, was published by NeoPoiesis Press in 2009 as well as his second poetry collection *Nirvana Haymaker* in 2012. His third poetry collection, *Blood Music*, was published by Punk Hostage Press in 2013. In 2014 Reardon published a chapbook with Dog On A Chain Press titled *The Broken Halo Blues*. Frank is currently working on short fiction, and a novel.

**Kevin Ridgeway** lives and writes in Long Beach, CA. Recent work has appeared in *Chiron Review*, *Nerve Cowboy*, *Trailer Park Quarterly* and *Spillway*, among others. His latest chapbook, *Contents Under Pressure*, is now available from Crisis Chronicles Press.

**Andy Roberts**, a four time Pushcart Prize nominee, lives in Columbus, Ohio where he handles finances for disabled veterans. Recent publications include *Atlanta Review*, *Chiron Review*, *The Midwest Quarterly*, *Mudfish*, *Slipstream*, and *Tule Review*. His latest chapbook, *Yeasayer*, was published by Night Ballet Press in 2016.

162

**Sam Robertson** grew up in St. Catharines, Ontario and now lives in Brooklyn, NY. He loves to spend time with family in The White Mountains of New Hampshire. His latest publications include poems in *The Hollins Critic*, *The Raintown Review*, and *The Same*.

**Philip Schaefer's** debut collection *Bad Summon* won the Agha Shahid Ali Poetry Prize from the University of Utah Press and will be released in 2017. He is the author of three chapbooks, two of which were co-written with friend and poet Jeff Whitney. He won the 2016 *Meridian* Editor's Prize in poetry and has individual work out or due out in *Kenyon Review, Thrush, Guernica, The Cincinnati Review, Birdfeast, Salt Hill, Bat City, Adroit, Baltimore Review,* and *Passages North* among others. He tends bar in Missoula, MT.

**Nancy Scott**, managing editor of *U.S.1 Worksheets*, journal of the U.S.1 Poets' Cooperative in New Jersey, is the author of nine collections of poetry, her most recent, *Ah, Men* (Aldrich Press, 2016) is a retrospective of men who have influenced her life. www.nancyscott.net

**Naomi Shihab Nye** was elected a Chancellor of the Academy of American Poets in 2009. Her latest book is *the Turtle of Oman*, a novel awarded a 2015 Middle East Book Award.

**Ciara Shuttleworth** was born in San Francisco and grew up in Nebraska, Nevada, and Washington state. Her poetry has been published in journals and anthologies, including *Alaska Quarterly Review, Confrontation, Hayden's Ferry Review, The New Yorker, The Norton Introduction to Literature 11e, Ploughshares,* and *The Southern Review*. Shuttleworth received an MFA in poetry from University of Idaho, a BFA in painting/drawing from San Francisco Art Institute, and a BA in studio art from Gustavus Adolphus College. She was The Jack Kerouac Project of Orlando's 51st resident at Jack Kerouac House. Shuttleworth's poetry chapbook, *Night Holds Its Own* (Blue Horse Press), is now available, and her gonzo prose book, *4500 Miles: Taking Jack Back on the Road* (Humanitas Media Publishing), was published in September, 2016. Her website is www.ciarashuttleworth.com.

**Danny Earl Simmons** is an Oregonian and a proud graduate of Corvallis High School. He is a friend of the Linn-Benton Community College Poetry Club and currently serves on the school's Poetry Advisory Committee. He is the author of a poetry chapbook entitled "The Allness of Everything" (Maverick Duck Press). He also assists the literary journal *Off the Coast* as a member of its editorial team.

**Michael Dwayne Smith** lives near a Mojave Desert ghost town with his family and rescued animals. Twice nominated for the Pushcart Prize, recipient of both the Hinderaker Award for poetry and Polonsky Prize for fiction, his work appears in 150+ publications, including *Cortland Review*, *Pirene's Fountain*, *Word Riot*, *Chiron Review*, *New World Writing*, *Heav*, *Feather Review*, *WhiskeyPaper*, and Heron Tree.

Costa Rican-American poet **Mark Smith-Soto** has been editor or associate editor of *International Poetry Review* at the University of North Carolina at Greensboro for over twenty years. Along with three prize-winning chapbooks he has authored three full-length poetry collections, *Our Lives Are Rivers* (University Press of Florida, 2003), *Any Second Now* (Main Street Rag Publishing Co., 2006) and *Time Pieces* (Main Street Rag Publishing Co., 2015). His work, which has appeared in *Antioch Review*, *Kenyon Review*, *Literary Review*, *Nimrod*, *Rattle*, *The Sun* and many other publications, has been nominated several times for a Pushcart Prize and was recognized in 2006 with an NEA Fellowship in Creative Writing. His *Fever Season: Selected Poetry of Ana Istarú* (2010) and his lyrical memoir *Berkeley Prelude* (2013) were both published by Unicorn Press.

**Brett Taylor** has published writing on cinema-related topics for *Filmfax* and *The South Carolina Review*. He has published photograph in *Big Muddy* and *Green Mountains Review*. He has been a tiger keeper, a farm worker, a factory worker, and a part time poker player. He lives in Tennessee.

**David E. Thomas** has published five books of poems, *Old Power Company Road* (2016), *Fossil Fuel, Buck's Last Wreck, The Hellgate Wind* and *Waterworks Hill*. He has poems in the anthologies *The Last Best Place* and *Poems across the Big Sky* and *New Poets of the American West* and has recently published poems in Romania, *Blue Collar Review* and *Cedilla 6, 7* and *8*. He currently lives in Missoula, Montana.

**Larry D. Thomas**, a member of the Texas Institute of Letters and the 2008 Texas Poet Laureate, has published several award-winning collections of poetry including *As If Light Actually Matters: New & Selected Poems* which received a 2015 Writers' League of Texas Book Awards Finalist citation. His most recent book of poems is *Bleak Music: Photographs and Poems of the American Southwest* (Blue Horse Press) which pairs twenty of his poems with the brilliant photographs of Jeffrey C. Alfier, publisher and co-editor of the *San Pedro River Review*. Thomas lives in the high

Chihuahuan Desert of Far West Texas with his wife and two long-haired Chihuahuas. Among his best friends are the Chihuahuan raven, puma, great horned owl, coyote, javelina, mule deer, gray fox, Texas horned lizard, thick-handed scorpion, black-tailed jackrabbit, diamondback rattlesnake, and blue quail.

**Robert Tremmel** lives and writes in Ankeny, Iowa. Recently, he's published in *Timberline Review*, *Poet Lore*, *Spillway*, *Packingtown Review*, *Roanoke Review*, *The Fourth River*, *Edge*, and others. He's also published two collections and a Chapbook titled *There is a Naked Man*.

**Gail Tyson** has published recent poetry and prose in *Art Ascent*, *Kindred*, *Punctuate*, *Still: the Journal*, and *Still Point Arts Quarterly*. She is an alumna of Rivendell Writers Colony, two College Institute writing workshops, and the Dylan Thomas Summer School at University of Wales.

**Jay Udall's** work has appeared in publications such as *North American Review*, *Beloit Poetry Journal*, *Verse Daily*, *Rattle*, *Prairie Schooner*, and *San Pedro River Review*. His fifth, latest volume of poems, *The Welcome Table*, won the New Mexico Book Award. He teaches at Nicholls State University in Thibodaux, Louisiana, where he also serves as poet-in-residence and chief editor of the online journal *Gris-Gris*.

**Michele Waering** spent her early years in the United States. She has an MLitt in Creative Writing from The University of Glasgow. Her work has been published in *From Glasgow to Saturn*; *From Quill to Quark; A Thousand Cranes: Scottish Poets for Japan*; *Envoi*; *The Interpreter's House*; *Red River Review*; *World Haiku Review* and *The Ghazal Page*. She lives in Renfrewshire, Scotland.

**Ron Wallace**, is an adjunct professor of English at Southeastern Oklahoma State University and an Oklahoma Native of Choctaw, Cherokee and Osage ancestry. He is the author of six volumes of poetry published by TJMF Publishing of Clarksville, Indiana and a three time finalist in the Oklahoma Book Awards. He is also a three time winner of The Oklahoma Writer's Federation Best Book of Poetry Award and a Pushcart Prize nominee for 2016. His work has been recently featured in *Oklahoma Today*, *Poetry Bay*, *Concho River Review*, *cybersoleil journal*, *Cobalt*, *Red Earth Review*, *Dragon Poets Review*, *Songs of Eretz Review*, *Gris-Gris*, *Oklahoma Poems and Their Poets* and a number of other magazines and anthologies.

**Jeff Whitney** is the author of *The Tree With Lights in it*, available from Thrush Press, while *Radio Silence* (Black Lawrence Press) and *Smoke*

*Tones* (Phantom Books) were co-written with poet Philip Schaefer. His poems can be found in journals such as *Adroit, Beloit Poetry Journal, Blackbird, Colorado Review, Narrative, Poetry Northwest,* and *Verse Daily.* He lives in Portland, where he teaches English.

**A.D. Winans** is an award winning native San Francisco poet and writer. H is the former editor/publisher of *Second Coming.* He is the author of over 60 books of poetry and prose. His latest book, *On My Way to Becoming a Man,* was published in 2014 by NYQ press. In 2006 he won a PEN Josephine Miles award for excellence in literature. In 2009 PEN Oakland presented him with a lifetime achievement award.

**Clarence Wolfshohl** has been active in the small press as writer and publisher for nearly fifty years. He has published poetry and non-fiction in many journals, both print and online, most recently, the e-chapbook *Scattering Ashes* (Virtual Artists Collective). Wolfshohl lives in the suburbs of Toledo, Missouri, with his dog and cat.

## Straight Ahead

Poems

Red Shuttleworth

Red Shuttleworth's Straight Ahead shows readers a crisply-drawn textual landscape of the scablands of Eastern Washington. This is a wounded land pocked with volcanic rock, coyotes, and "plow-ripped floury soil" that, like the mythic Old West, "declines and crumbles / blue rock suburban driveway gravel" and "double-wide farmhouses." In these stark and masterfully-wrought scenes—most crafted in chiseled tanka-like five-line poems—we get a glimpse into this microcosm of America through Shuttleworth's astute, terse, and always human observations. In Straight Ahead we hear the twenty-first century lament of the exile in the Western wilderness.

— Barbara Brinson Curiel, author, Mexican Jenny and Other Poems, winner of the 2012 Philip Levine Prize

$16.00. Paperback. 136 pages (January, 2017).

Available on Amazon.com

# Revenant

Poems

Jack B. Bedell

I have long admired Jack Bedell's poetry and count him as one of the South's most important poets. In this collection, *Revenant*, Bedell twines a water motif through each of these imaginal and imaginative poems. Indeed, what I most appreciate about Bedell's work is that, in what Robert Penn Warren called a "moment of mania," a moment inarguably still taking place in contemporary writing via the amorphous and befuddling poetry that predominates, Bedell's work is as clear and as important as air, but never airy, and his use of the elements— light, wind, and particularly water—ensure that these poems will exist in readers' minds long after they've been read. Bedell focuses on the important and the radiant.

— William Wright, Series Editor, *The Southern Poetry Anthology*

$10.00. Paperback. 40 pages (November, 2016)

Available on Amazon.com

New from 2009 *SPRR* issue Contributor Alan King

## Excerpts

"Weren't you naive once, thinking
all there was to keeping a woman
was breaking the last man's record
while she cried out,
then kissed you afterwards?

That's when you were young enough
to see the climax as a finish line
you bolted across before collapsing,
breathless and disoriented,
like the couple upstairs
whose sounds slide down
to you and your sleeping wife..."
-from "At The High Point"

"A woman's yell calls me back
across the street. It's the neighbor
on her front porch, wearing
a blue tattered housecoat
and floppy pink slippers.

She holds up her phone,
and the crowd scatters,
*Y'all need to stop! I got police on the line!*

I wish I had someone like her
to save me from myself..."
-from "Swarm"

# New from the Blue Horse Press Editors

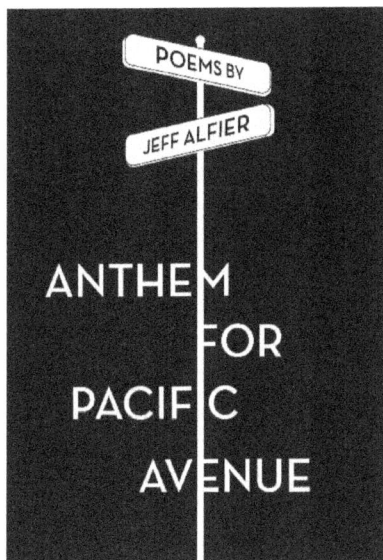

Jeffrey Alfier's gaze is empathic and disarming. The working poor and social outcasts are given a home in deftly-honed stanzas. Highways, hotel rooms, and bars become both holy and profane spaces. His attentiveness to the distance between people is instructive, tender. His language blazes with insight and grace.

— Eduardo C. Corral

Cowboy Buddha Publishing. $14.95. Paperback. 54 pages (February, 2017).

Available on Amazon.com

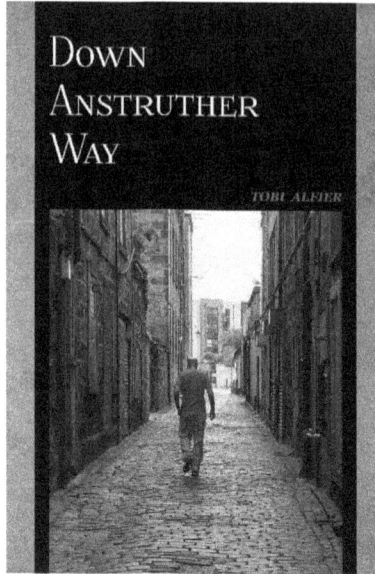

Tobi takes us on her journey of love and into a Scotland of hard work, pubs, lorries, lochs. We jaunt with her through her embrace of Scottish life which unfolds with such words as wellies, crofts, keening, jammy, Angus, loch and of course Anstruther. Many phrases skillfully evoke a scene or circumstance - "an audience of clouds," "she has been widowed forever," "lives ordained by obligation," "radar antennas that whisk like a bowl of creamy cloud." One doesn't just read *Down Anstruther Way*, one accompanies Tobi on her journey of love and Scotland. Join her.

— Peter Krok

FutureCycle Press. $11.95. Paperback. 38 pages (December, 2016).

Available on Amazon.com

www.ingramcontent.com/pod-product-compliance
Lightning Source LLC
Chambersburg PA
CBHW051727040426
42447CB00008B/1002